Docto

Divine in Show

T. McALINDON

*W*hat art thou, Faustus, but a man condemned to *die?* With his famous play *Doctor Faustus* (1592), Elizabethan dramatist Christopher Marlowe (1564–1593) brilliantly staged the story of a renowned scholar who sells his soul to the Devil in exchange for magical powers. Marlowe's Faustus is the classic character who shuns God's graces and the prospect of heavenly bliss in order to pass his mortal years "in all voluptuousness"—only to suffer harrowing despair at the threshold of eternal damnation. As T. McAlindon shows in this beautifully written and exceptionally well versed study, Marlowe's masterwork so vividly articulates the Christian fear of Hell, the human struggle against earthly temptation, and the longing for God's mercy, that it inspired new Faustus stories by Lessing, Goethe, and Mann, and influenced writers from Shakespeare to Conrad. Marlowe's drama has also taken a significant place in Western popular thought: as McAlindon leads us through its five acts, we see that many now-familiar ideas—the devil-pact signed in blood, the conflicting voices of Good and Bad Angels, God's exile of Lucifer, the treachery of Satan's agent Mephistopheles, and the inexorable ruin of a soul gone astray—were first brought to life in Marlowe's *Doctor Faustus.*

McAlindon delves into the mind of Marlowe—an arrogantly rebellious freethinker who might have been imprisoned for atheism if he hadn't first been killed in a barroom brawl—and explores the playwright's fascination with the ambition, godlessness, and final despair of his hero. Both Marlowe and Faustus, McAlindon reveals, are caught in the turbulent cross-currents of the Reformation: both paid the Medieval price of spiritual terror for living by the Renaissance ideals of humanism and high aspiration. Following McAlindon through Marlowe's rich weave of emotion, poetry, drama, irony, and symbolism, we explore such pivotal scenes as Faustus's first summoning of Mephistopheles, his travels with Mephistopheles through the cosmos and their insult to the Pope, his conjuring of fantastic images to delight the aristocracy and to cheat a common horse-trader, and his magical resurrection of Helen of Troy.

DOCTOR FAUSTUS

Divine in Show

TWAYNE'S MASTERWORK STUDIES

Robert Lecker, General Editor

DOCTOR FAUSTUS

Divine in Show

T. McAlindon

TWAYNE PUBLISHERS • NEW YORK
Maxwell Macmillan Canada • *Toronto*
Maxwell Macmillan International • *New York Oxford Singapore Sydney*

Twayne's Masterwork Series No. 134

Doctor Faustus: Divine in Show
Thomas McAlindon

Twayne Publishers
Macmillan Publishing Company
866 Third Avenue
New York, New York 10022

Maxwell Macmillan Canada, Inc.
1200 Eglinton Avenue East
Suite 200
Don Mills, Ontario M3C 3N1

Library of Congress Cataloging-in-Publication Data

McAlindon, T. (Thomas)
    Doctor Faustus : divine in show / Thomas McAlindon.
        p.   cm.—(Twayne's masterwork studies; no. 134)
    Includes bibliographical references and index.
    ISBN 0-8057-4453-3 (alk. paper)—ISBN 0-8057-8388-1 (pbk.: alk. paper)
    1. Marlowe, Christopher, 1564–1593. Doctor Faustus. 2. Faust, d.
    ca. 1540—In literature. 3. Magician in literature. 4. Tragedy.
    I. Title. II. Series
    PR2664.M37   1994
    822'.3—dc20   94-16635
                                                                              CIP

10 9 8 7 6 5 4 3 2 1 (hc)
10 9 8 7 6 5 4 3 2 1 (pb)

Printed in the United States of America

To Margot,
again

Contents

Putative portrait of Christopher Marlowe. *Reproduced by permission of the Master, Fellows, and Scholars of Corpus Christi College, Cambridge.*

Illustrations

Note on the References
and Acknowledgments

Doctor Faustus has come down to us in two forms, the A text of 1604 and the B text of 1616. The B text is an amplified and slightly altered version of the A text (or its source); presumably it contains the additions that the theatrical financier Philip Henslowe commissioned William Birde and Samuel Rowley to write in 1602. Scholarly and critical preference has oscillated between the two texts, but at present there is a marked shift of opinion in favor of the A text. In this book, I have used Roma Gill's New Mermaid edition (New York: Norton; London: Black, 2d ed., 1989); it is based on the A text but has an appendix containing those scenes from the B text that are either "straightforward additions to the play presented in the A text" or "have been substantially reworked" (69). I am not inclined to believe, as some now claim, that the B text is either inferior to, or conspicuously different in meaning from, the A text, or both. In fact, I am impressed by the way in which the B-text additions and variations show a sensitive understanding of the pattern of ideas, images, and motifs that inheres in the shorter version. The B text, in my view, offers the first and in some ways the best interpretation of Marlowe's play.

Thus, although my own commentary is firmly based on the play as given in Gill's A-text edition, I have, from time to time and with due specification, cited additional evidence from the B text in a manner intended both to register my respect for that text and to reinforce my own reading of the A text. In this way, I hope to provide an account of the play that is not seriously affected by the textual dispute—a dispute that, despite current certainties, is unlikely ever to achieve a lasting settlement. The B-text material in Gill's appendix has no lineation; my quotations from this material, therefore, are followed only by a page reference (thus, B.85). Citations of B-text material not given in Gill's appendix are from Greg's parallel edition of the two texts and are followed by line reference (thus: Greg, 280). Citations of Gill's A text are followed by scene and line reference (thus, "2.109" is scene 2, line 109) or chorus and line reference ("chor.4.6" is chorus 4, line 6).

I should like to thank Rowland Wymer and Robin Headlam Wells for the care with which they scrutinized what I have written here, eliminating errors and blemishes, and making fruitful suggestions.

Chronology: Christopher Marlowe's Life and Works

1558	Accession of Elizabeth I.
1564	Shakespeare born. Marlowe born in Canterbury to shoemaker John Marlowe and wife, Katherine. Marlowe's father is gregarious, forceful, quarrelsome, and improvident; well acquainted with debt and the law.
1568–1572	Catholic opposition to Elizabeth, supported by Spain and the pope, culminating in the unsuccessful Northern Revolt. Seven hundred Catholics executed.
1573	Elizabeth makes peace with Spain. Beginning of a period of maritime and commercial expansion abroad and of industrial development at home.
1578	English privateering and military support for Philip's rebellious Protestant subjects in the Netherlands renew Spain's hostility to Elizabeth. Marlowe becomes a scholar at King's School, Canterbury, his fees probably paid for by charity or patronage.
1581	First of several Catholic plots against Elizabeth's life uncovered. Penal laws against Catholics enacted.
1580	Sir Francis Drake returns in triumph from his voyage round the world, laden with Spanish plunder. Marlowe is awarded an Archbishop Parker scholarship and begins his studies at Corpus Christi College, Cambridge.
1583	Archbishop Whitgift begins his "inquisition" against Puritan dissent, whose intellectual center is Cambridge University.
1584	Marlowe passes his B.A. examinations. Remains on scholarship at Cambridge for two more years, presumably on condition that he will proceed to holy orders.

1585	England goes to war with Spain in the Netherlands. *Dido and Aeneas*, thought to be Marlowe's first play.
1587	Execution of Mary, Queen of Scots, Catholic claimant to Elizabeth's throne. Expedition of Sir Francis Drake to "singe the King of Spain's beard." Cambridge University refuses to award Marlowe the M.A., irritated, perhaps, by his abandonment of a clerical career, but also suspecting him of Catholic sympathies and of visits to the English Catholic seminary in Rheims, France. The Queen's Privy Council intervenes instructing the University to award him the degree; he has been "employed . . . in matters touching the benefit of his country"—possibly spying on English Catholics abroad. Secret agent Marlowe gets his M.A. Probably in this year, too, he captivates London audiences with his drama of heroic conquest, *Tamburlaine the Great*. Its success leads promptly to a sequel, *Tamburlaine Part II*.
1588	Spain attacks England. Defeat of the Great Armada, but the threat of invasion persists, and England remains at war with Spain until after Elizabeth's death.
1589	Marlowe and his friend Thomas Watson, the poet, are involved in a fight with one William Bradley in Hog Lane, London. Watson kills Bradley. Both Marlowe and Watson are imprisoned but successfully plead self-defense.
c. 1589	*The Jew of Malta*, Marlowe's tragedy of Machiavellian intrigue and religious conflict.
1591	Marlowe shares a room with dramatist Thomas Kyd, author of the popular and influential *The Spanish Tragedy* (c. 1585–90). After Marlowe's death, Kyd will describe him as "intemperate and of a cruel heart," prompt to deliver "sudden privy injuries to men," and shockingly irreligious.
c. 1591	Marlowe's historical tragedy with a homosexual hero, *Edward II*.
1592	In January, Marlowe is arrested in Flushing (an English possession on the Dutch coast) and sent back to England on a charge of counterfeiting, the evidence against him supplied by his chamber-fellow, Richard Baines. He and Baines accuse each other of intending to join England's Catholic enemies abroad. Nothing comes of these charges. In May, Marlowe is arrested in London for breaking the peace; he is bound over for the sum of £20. In September, writer Robert Greene pens a deathbed pamphlet in which he laments that Marlowe, "famous gracer of tragedians," is blinded by "diabolical athe-

ism," and warns that he will find in "that liberty . . . an infernal bondage." In September–October in Canterbury, Marlowe is charged with assaulting William Corkine "with staff and dagger." After a cooling period, Corkine drops the charge.

1592–1593   *Doctor Faustus* probably written and first performed about this time. (Some scholars favor an earlier date.)

1593   In January, first performance of Marlowe's topical anti-Catholic tragedy on religious conflict in France, *The Massacre at Paris*. On 11 May, Kyd is arrested on suspicion of libelous activities and interrogated under torture on the rack; allegedly heretical writings are discovered in his room, but he claims they belonged to Marlowe. Letters written later by Kyd suggest that under torture he also accuses Marlowe at this time of making heretical and treasonable statements. The Privy Council issues a warrant for Marlowe's arrest. On 20 May, Marlowe gets off lightly, being ordered to make a daily appearance before the council until their lordships decide otherwise. Marlowe spends 30 May feasting with three companions in Deptford. He quarrels over payment of the bill with Ingram Frizer. Approaching the seated Frizer from behind, he pulls out Frizer's dagger and strikes him, probably with the handle. Frizer grapples with him and in the tussle the dagger enters Marlowe's skull above the eye. He dies immediately. (There have been several theories that Marlowe's death was politically contrived rather than accidental.) Possibly on 2 June, unaware of Marlowe's death, Richard Baines delivers his famous note to the Privy Council, giving a detailed summary of the atheistical, heretical, blasphemous, and treasonable opinions to which Marlowe, he claims, gave regular and uninhibited utterance. On 29 June, professional informer and government spy Richard Cholmley accuses Marlowe of being expert in atheistic arguments and of telling him "he gave the atheist lecture to Sir Walter Ralegh and others." Baines's note may be a rough summary of this lecture.

1594   Publication of *Edward II* and *The Tragedy of Dido, Queen of Carthage*. Released from prison, Thomas Kyd dies a broken man, abandoned by his aristocratic patrons and in debt.

1598   Publication of Marlowe's *Hero and Leander*, an unfinished love poem.

1599   Marlowe's translations from the Latin of Ovid's erotic poems, the *Amores*, are among books publicly burnt on the orders of the archbishop of Canterbury and the bishop of London.

	Written perhaps during his Cambridge days, these translations were probably published shortly before they were condemned.
1600	Publication of *The First Book of Lucan*, Marlowe's translation from Lucan's epic on the civil wars of Caesar and Pompey. Possibly another Cambridge composition.
1603	Death of Queen Elizabeth and accession of James I.

LITERARY AND HISTORICAL CONTEXT

1

Renaissance and Reformation

As the reign of James I progressed, many of his disillusioned subjects began to look back nostalgically to the age of "good Queen Bess." They saw there a stable, prosperous, and unified nation ruled by an upright and dignified monarch, and a court that was justly admired throughout Europe for its splendor and decorum. There was a core of substantial truth in this conception, but as my brief chronology should indicate, it was an utterly simplified conception, too. The foundations of Elizabethan society were insecure from the beginning of the period to the end. Its cohesion was due in large measure to the continued threat of invasion and to the harsh repression of internal dissent. Its sumptuously elegant court was a place of hungry ambition and Machiavellian intrigue. At the center of this court was a conscientious Christian ruler who regularly resorted to ruthless and cunning strata-gems in defense of her regime; she was a learned queen, too, who accepted plunder from piratical adventurers with unashamed grati-tude: "Arise, Sir Francis. . . ."

Christopher Marlowe's life and works assuredly reflect the con-tradictions of this extraordinary time, for here was a scholar and intended clergyman who engaged in espionage and frequented the seedy underworld of Elizabethan informers. He was an obedient servant of the Protestant state and an arrogantly rebellious freethinker, a greatly imaginative writer, and a fatally compulsive brawler. His plays bear witness in equal measure to an intense and refined love of beauty and to a fascination with violence and cruelty. They celebrate exuberant self-expression, and they ironically unfold the self-destructive folly and inevitable punishment of untrammeled individualism. Marlowe's sudden, violent death preempted an appearance before the Privy Council that could have had frightening consequences. It is almost as if in dramatizing the rebellion and damnation of Faustus he was offloading a personal nightmare, shadowing forth a nocturnal apprehension of his own present and future state. The relationship between his work, his life, and his time was one of intricate and, in the end, uncanny intimacy.

The most distinctive features of the Elizabethan period—its achievements, its contradictions, and its tensions—can be explained in large measure, and with some simplification, in terms of two great cultural movements, the Renaissance and the Reformation. Affecting England (like Spain) much later than Italy, the Renaissance signified an awakening of imaginative, intellectual, and social energies based on a return to classical literature and the moral and aesthetic values it enshrined. It entailed a turning away from medieval asceticism, with its contempt for the body, its ideal of humility, and its insistence that the world is but a vale of tears where the soul prepares for happiness in the afterlife. What the Renaissance fostered was a new regard for the individual, for human potential, for natural beauty and the emotions, and for the joys and pleasures of this world. Inverting a cherished medieval hierarchy, it exalted the life of action—the life of man and woman in society—over the life of contemplation and retreat. In short, the Renaissance provided a secularized view of life. Many sober minds felt that it constituted a pagan threat to Christian belief and practice, but the leading Christian humanists—those scholars who masterminded the study of classical texts and the propagation of classical ideals—were sincerely convinced that the two cultural traditions were fundamentally compatible. They promoted a form of education that combined religious and humanistic studies, developed moral and

4

aesthetic awareness, and prepared the student for life in a civilized society.

A central feature of Renaissance education, both at school and university, was the study of rhetoric as taught by the great Roman masters Cicero and Quintilian. Students were drilled in the art of disputation and in the choice and fashioning of styles appropriate to every subject and occasion. Speaking well—eloquence—was the aim, and its purpose was to equip students for public office and, more generally, to help them negotiate the multifarious circumstances of life in a ceremonious, hierarchical society. Both at school and university, rhetorical training was reinforced by the performance of plays, which perfected the arts of memory and delivery. Rhetoric and drama are natural allies, and the combined effect of their contribution to Renaissance education was to intensify the theatricality of social life, the conviction that all the world's a stage, where success depends on how well we play our appointed or chosen role. Rhetorical education, too, provided a perfect context for the nurturing of dramatic talent, developing as it did not only a mastery of different styles and voices but also the dialectical frame of mind, which delights in the interaction of opposing viewpoints. Drama, as the French critic Brunetiére has said, is the art of conflict.

The more fervent representatives of the Reformation were deeply hostile to theatricality and eloquence, associating them with the delusive arts of the devil and the showiness of Roman Catholicism. After decades of vituperation against the stage, the Puritans eventually closed the English theaters in 1642; in the pulpit they replaced Latinate grandeur with native plainness. In general, the Reformation did much to cool the ardors and enfeeble the optimism released by the Renaissance. Whereas the humanists emphasized the dignity of human nature and man's capacity to win salvation for his soul through reason and divine revelation, Calvin and Luther preached the utter degradation of fallen human nature and the total incapacity of mortals to save themselves from the damnation that they so thoroughly deserve. Whereas humanists regarded human beings as free to choose what they will become, Luther and Calvin saw them as miserable creatures in bondage to Satan and the law and insisted that those who are

5

released from such bondage owe their liberation to the entirely unmerited gift of divine grace. The central doctrine of the reformed church was justification by faith: "works" (implicitly associated with the prescribed rituals of the Catholic church) accomplish nothing; only faith in divine grace can save the soul from eternal punishment. This humbling doctrine was closely tied to the terrifying doctrine of election, according to which God, in his unfathomable justice, has predestined from the beginning those who will be saved (a very small minority) and those who will be damned.

The political troubles of Elizabeth's reign, and most of the bitter constraints endured by her subjects, are bound up with the effects of the Reformation. Elizabeth inherited a nation confused and divided after the committed Protestantism of Edward's reign (1547–53) and the relentless Catholicism of Mary's (1553–58). As head of the established church of England, Elizabeth sought to effect a unifying compromise between the old and the new but could satisfy neither the Catholics nor her own radical co-religionists. The Catholics in the North revolted and paid a huge price. Pope Pius V condemned Elizabeth as a heretic and usurper, released Catholics from their oath of fealty, and so legitimized attempts to assassinate and replace her. Thus, patriotism became synonymous with Protestantism, crippling fines were imposed on practicing Catholics, and missionary priests were subjected to tortures and executions as horrific as any devised by our modern experts. The prolonged war with Spain, the external corollary to this intestine conflict, drained the economy and contributed greatly to the poverty and discontent that characterized the last decade of the century.

Meanwhile, the Puritans (the most important of whom came from Marlowe's university) contended that the church had yet to cleanse itself of its residual popery. Rites and ceremonies—all that theatrical display, as Calvin called it—must go, and so, too, must the hierarchical mode of government embodied in episcopal rule. Knowing that most of her Protestant subjects were attached to the ceremonial content of their religion and, more important, knowing that "no bishop" ultimately would mean "no king," Elizabeth was unrelenting in her resistance to these calls. The full coercive power of the state was brought to bear on dissenting Protestants. Uncompliant bishops and clergy were suspended, sentences of exile and even death could be passed on those who refused to attend church, and parliamentary discussion of religious matters was forbidden. And of course the great, quasi-autonomous machine of state suspicion, arbitrary imprisonment, and systematic torture—that terrible machine in which poor Thomas Kyd was cruelly caught and which would probably have broken Marlowe had he lived—did its work, providing "guilty" and "innocent" alike with their taste of hell on earth.

Doctor Faustus is a tragedy of soaring, lyrical aspiration, rebellious pride, degrading constriction, physical and spiritual terror, and paralyzing despair. It takes little imagination to see it as an authentic product of this historical period.

2

Marlowe's Myth

Of the six surviving plays written by Marlowe, *Doctor Faustus* is by far the most famous, yet it is by no means the most finished and satisfactory. It is indeed depressingly uneven, so that scholars have long surmised that much of it (and not just the additions paid for by Philip Henslowe in 1602) was written by a collaborator or collaborators of greatly inferior capacities. Yet, the overall conception of the tragedy is superb, and those parts of it that are unquestionably by Marlowe show him at his greatest as a poetic dramatist. Nowhere else does he communicate so much with such economy; nowhere else is his emotional intensity or his dramatic irony so piercing.

Doctor Faustus is a remarkable and fascinating play for a number of other reasons. In the first place, it is the only major play on a religious theme produced for the stage in that profoundly religious epoch; perhaps only a "proud, audacious" genius such as Marlowe would undertake such a theme at a time when religion was so dangerously sensitive an issue. That Marlowe, the notorious scorner of established religious beliefs, should not only undertake to dramatize the story but also forcefully equate Faustus's revolt with blind folly and foreground eternal damnation as an inescapable reality is a most intriguing paradox. Perhaps it was precisely his loss of the faith he once held that made it possible for Marlowe to achieve so extraordinary a combination of imaginative commitment to, and detachment from, the given theme.

What makes the play most remarkable is the fact that in composing it Marlowe so elicited the latent meanings of the devil compact—a type of story that had been familiar in the West for centuries—that he gave it the force and status of myth. Indeed, he shaped it into a myth that usurped the place in the Western imagination hitherto enjoyed by the myths of Lucifer and of Adam and Eve. The Faust figure has become the archetype of all human striving to reach beyond the human; more particularly, he has become the personification of that postmedieval phenomenon we call individualism.

The play began to assume an archetypal dimension in the seventeenth century. Although it did not generate other religious tragedies, its tragic structure and mythic force left their mark on a number of major Renaissance plays. Among these, the most notable are Shakespeare's *Macbeth* (1606) and Thomas Middleton and William Rowley's *The Changeling* (1622). What both of these plays seem to have inherited from *Doctor Faustus* is the structuring, ironic concept of the fatal "deed." A deliberate act or choice, the deed is a deed in two senses of the word, since it confronts the doer with the fact that there is no such thing as autonomy of action in the real world: every act has binding consequences. Whereas the protagonist believes that the rebellious deed will give him complete freedom and fulfillment, it brings minimal satisfaction and quickly leads to a state of humiliating dependence. Every attempt to undo it or to avoid its effects simply results in a state of ever greater commitment to evil and constitutes another step on the path of spiritual enslavement and self-destruction. This ironic structure generates questions about the paradoxical relationship between limit and freedom; about the nature and effects of evil; about the freedom, corruption, and bondage of the will; about the way in which despair and desperation will drive individuals endowed with moral sense beyond the boundaries that distinguish the human from the bestial and the demonic.

The next major developments in the interpretation of the myth take place in Germany, where the historical Faust and his legend originated. The *Historia von D. Johann Fausten* (1587) was a popular piece of sensational folk fiction (or chapbook) in that country. But Marlowe's play was acted and well known in Germany in the seventeenth century, and it would seem to have been that version of the story that impressed its possibilities on sophisticated minds such as Lessing in the eighteenth century and Goethe in the nineteenth. With these two great writers the motivation of Faust's revolt alters somewhat, but more important, the authorial attitude to that revolt undergoes a radical change, so that one begins to see that this is a myth in which each age will comment—adversely, ambiguously, or positively—on its own aspirations and achievements.

Marlowe's protagonist scorned human limitations in search of power, pleasure, and knowledge; Macbeth sought power and also knowledge of a special, nonintellectual kind (the witches' "more . . . than mortal knowledge" (1.5.2) of the future). In *The Changeling*, Beatrice-Joanna disregarded all moral constraints in the pursuit of sexual satisfaction. Lessing's Faust, however, is driven by an insatiable intellectual curiosity, and nothing else. In keeping with the temper of the Age of Enlightenment, this kind of desire to transcend human limitations is seen as entirely laudable, so that Faust, although erring, is saved. In Goethe's *Faust*, the boundless desire is not only for knowledge but also for experience: a desire to do all that it is possible for human beings to do. This, too, is seen as intrinsically noble, a manifestation not only of romantic individualism but also of the nineteenth-century commitment to the idea of progress. So Goethe's hero, too, is saved, moving toward salvation—or, rather, apotheosis—by gradually shaking off his ruthless egoism and acquiring positive, humanitarian attitudes inspired by the love of nature and classical notions of harmony and beauty.

Among the numerous versions of the Faust myth produced in the nineteenth century, most follow the salvationist pattern. In the disillusionment of the twentieth century—which has produced as large a crop of Faust figures as the nineteenth—the mythical rebel has predictably reassumed his darker, tragic status. While damnation is not an issue in any literal sense, its symbolic significance as an irreversible loss of innocence, integrity, and spiritual freedom is operative. Like so much else in twentieth-century thought, this development was anticipated by Friedrich Nietzsche in the nineteenth century. In *The Birth of Tragedy* (1872), Nietzsche construed Faust as prototypal modern man, exploring every sphere of knowledge and then driven by dissatisfaction to make a pact with the powers of darkness. And so, in Oswald Spengler's powerful essay in the philosophy of history, *The Decline of the West* (published a few months before the collapse of Germany in World War I), Faust personifies the whole motive force of modern culture: he is modern man in servitude to his technological inventions and trapped by his economic devices.

War, too, casts its shadow over Thomas Mann's massive novel *Doctor Faustus* (1947). Begun in the middle of World War II, it associates the myth with the triumph of sophisticated barbarism over humanistic culture in Germany during the two decades before 1930. But for the English-speaking world, perhaps the most impressive modern incarnation of the Faust myth is to be found in Joseph Conrad's *Heart of Darkness* (1899). The nineteenth-century dream of progress is here identified with colonialism and personified in the figure of the trader Kurtz. It is a dream that quickly becomes a nightmare. As the narrator Marlow discovers (and can the conjunction of Marlow's name and Kurtz's German name be mere coincidence?), Kurtz achieves godlike status, but only at the price of participating in demonic rites. He becomes enslaved to the barbarism that he thought he, as an emissary of civilization, would eradicate. He dies much like Faustus, contemplating "The horror! The horror!"

"How greatly is it all planned!" exclaimed Goethe, expressing his intense admiration for Marlowe's tragedy. Time has given that famous remark considerably more significance than Goethe intended. As shaped originally by Marlowe, "the form of Faustus' fortunes, good or bad" (*DF*, chor.1.8) bewitched the European mind.

3

Doctor Faustus and the Critics

Doctor Faustus was a great theatrical success in England from the time of its first performance until the closing of the theaters in 1642. It was probably never acted in England, and attracted almost no critical interest, throughout the eighteenth century. Although there is no recorded production of the play in the nineteenth century until the year 1895, it had long since become the best-known and most admired of all Renaissance plays outside Shakespeare. The age of romanticism, with its regard for rebellious individualism and emotional intensity and its attraction to supernatural and Satanic themes, saw it as a flawed but nonetheless magnificent dramatic poem. William Hazlitt (1820) set the style for romantic criticism when he identified Faustus with Marlowe and found in both "a lust of power . . . a glow of imagination, unhallowed by anything but its own energies," a "grand and daring" character who personifies "the pride of will and eagerness of curiosity sublimed beyond the reach of fear and remorse."[1] In his endeavor to present Faustus as the complete romantic hero, sublime alike in his aspirations and his courage, Hazlitt blandly misrepresented the unheroic feelings of regret and terror that were so memorably expressed in the last scene. At the end of the century we find A. C.

Swinburne engaged in exactly the same process of idealization and simplification.[2]

Not all nineteenth-century critics presented Faustus as a sublime Promethean hero or assumed that Marlowe wholeheartedly approved of his rebellion. Wilhelm Wagner (1877) insisted that since Faustus never derives any benefit from the Satanic pact, never becomes master of Mephistopheles, and devotes himself to childish pastimes, he is "anything but a hero" (*MDF*, 33). A. C. Bradley (1880) emphasized the "appalling" nature of the final scene and claimed that the greatness of the play lies not only in the volcanic self-assertion of its hero but also in the dramatist's insight into its significance and tragic results (*MCH*, 128). J. A. Symonds (1884) imputed artistic detachment and a complex tragic conception to Marlowe. While agreeing that Faustus is vitalized by much of Marlowe's own fiery sympathy, he insisted that Faustus's desire for the impossible is shown to put him in revolt against the laws of his own nature and of the world. Also, instead of seeing Faustus in terms of a preconceived heroic simplicity, Symonds emphasized "the perplexities of his divided spirit."[3]

But even Symonds and Bradley exemplify the common nineteenth-century habit (still in evidence today) of providing a homogenized portrait of the Marlovian hero and treating Faustus as the most attractive version of the common model. All the more notable therefore is W. J. Courthope's recognition (1895) that although "resolution"—the firmness of determined will—is, for Marlowe, the supreme quality, Faustus, unlike Tamburlaine and the Jew of Malta, does not possess it. His soul, like Hamlet's and Macbeth's, is torn between conflicting principles; for this reason, *Doctor Faustus* is Marlowe's most interesting play (*MCH*, 196–97).

Nevertheless, the romantic response to *Doctor Faustus* as an approving and heroic portrait of rebellious self assertion, and an affirmation of Marlowe's own values, persisted well into the twentieth century. Then came the recognition that this view has to accommodate contradiction and paradox. So, for George Santayana (1910), the devil is really intended to represent the good: he offers everything the Renaissance prized—power, knowledge, beauty, enterprise, wealth. Faustus is a martyr to these values and is damned, not because he is culpable, but by accident or predestination, or because he is carried "a bit too far" by ambition and pleasure (*MDF*, 39). Una Ellis-Fermor (1927) felt that if Marlowe had completed the play as he ought to have, he would not have damned Faustus but would have endorsed the Renaissance pride, aspiration, and love of beauty that Faustus shares with Tamburlaine; instead, Marlowe gave in to the ruthless side of his mind, which had been trained in a gloomy theology.[4]

Finally, in 1952, Nicholas Brooke sought to reinstate the heroic Faustus and to acknowledge the contradictory aspect of the play without impugning its author's artistic integrity. Marlowe, he claimed, deliberately misused the traditional morality form and the values it enshrined. He put conviction into the voice of hell, and not of heaven, and ensured that all the positive elements in the play would be against the declared Christian moral. Faustus's heroism lies precisely in his choice of what was traditionally considered evil and in his rejection of heaven as representing a way of life that is unworthy of him (*MDF*, 101–33). Here we have an interpretation that provocatively remodels the romantic hero in the light of Nietzsche's anti-Christian superman. It rests on the flat denial (*MDF*, 108) of the subtle ironies that everyone now acknowledges to be present in the Helen speech. It also disregards the fact that the most powerful and moving speeches in the tragedy—Mephistopheles's outburst "Why this is hell, nor am I out of it," and Faustus's final soliloquy—are premised on Christian doctrine.

Brooke was consciously resisting new trends. From around 1940 until 1980 most criticism of *Doctor Faustus* reflected the aims and interests of two methodologies: the New Criticism, with its emphasis on the autonomy of the text (irrespective of what we know or conjecture about the author) and its preoccupation with irony, ambiguity, and ambivalence; and historicism, with its assumption that the text must be studied in relation to all those aspects of its original cultural context that seem relevant to it. Thus, on the one hand came a decisive shift away from the romantic glorification of Faustus and the emergence of Marlowe as a detached dramatist who (whatever his own beliefs may have been) looks on his protagonist's rejection of God with more disapproval than approval, more irony than sympathy, and on the other hand, a recognition that the text is a site not only for

Renaissance ideas about human aspiration and beauty but also for Christian and, more specifically, Reformation teachings on sin, grace, repentance, and damnation. The antiromantic reaction began vigorously with James Smith (1939), who insisted that *Doctor Faustus* is a wholly orthodox Christian play and that romantic critics made the great mistake of reading it in the light of Goethe's *Faust*. Arguing that Faustus is justly damned for the sin of pride, Smith demonstrated the unity and coherence of the play by reference to the retrospective ironies embedded in the final soliloquy (*MDF*, 49–70). Leo Kirschbaum (1943) was even more emphatic when he insisted that Faustus is not Marlowe the atheist and that the Christian premises of the given story are endorsed throughout. Kirschbaum was the first to point out that Faustus's address to Helen of Troy, which earlier critics had construed as a perfect hymn to pagan beauty, is undercut by ironic ambiguities hinting at destruction and damnation. Marlowe's irony, according to Kirschbaum, exposes Faustus's rebellious pride as a compound of vanity, egocentricity, and folly.[5]

While not normally as harsh on Faustus as Kirschbaum and Smith were, many other critics developed the positions established by them. Among the more important were F. P. Wilson (1951) and Lily B. Campbell (1952), both of whom emphasized the tragic qualities of the play as well as its religious orthodoxy. For Wilson, the play was a genuine religious tragedy where the protagonist falls as the result of a freely chosen action, but his end excites pity and terror to a degree hitherto unknown on the English stage.[6] Like Wilson, Campbell focused on the theme of despair and linked the play to the famous case of Francis Spira, a Protestant who recanted his faith, repented his recantation, but despaired of God's mercy and committed suicide. Campbell also noted that such "cases of conscience" were commonplace in the religious literature of a period dominated by the doctrine of justification by faith. She contended that *Doctor Faustus* is best understood, not as a tragedy of Renaissance humanism, but as a Reformation tragedy of religious despair. Its effects of pity and terror arise from its overwhelming sense of the importance of what happens to Faustus's soul; its great suspense is due to the agonizing uncertainty about the final outcome of the action.[7]

W. W. Greg (1946) and Helen Gardner (1948) had noted the play's connection with the morality drama, a genre that flourished in the fifteenth and early sixteenth centuries and in which the plot turned on temptation, sin, and the imminence of death and possible damnation. Gardner also noted that the Spira case had been crudely dramatized in just this form by Nathaniel Woodes in 1581. Marlowe's use of morality conventions was fruitfully investigated in 1962 by both David Bevington and Douglas Cole. Bevington's work had the effect of reinforcing arguments in favor of the play's structural and thematic coherence. *Doctor Faustus*, he explained, dramatizes a spiritual biography from innocence to damnation according to the morality pattern of psychomachic conflict. Its alternation of serious and comic scenes, far from signifying artistic incoherence, is an inheritance from the morality tradition that serves to emphasize Faustus's spiritual decline.[8] For Cole, Faustus, like the "everyman" protagonist of the morality plays, reenacts the archetypal fall, which brought evil into the world by the abuse of freedom and by revolt against natural order; thus, Faustus is neither hero nor villain but Adamic man, willfully choosing destruction under the guise of self-glory.[9] Whereas Bevington saw a tension in *Doctor Faustus* between the values of tragedy and those of morality, for Cole (as for Wilson and Campbell) these two dimensions apparently formed a balanced unity.

Tragedy (or *heroic tragedy*) and *morality* became the two rubrics under which the interpretive and evaluative problems presented by the play were commonly discussed. For the notion of the play as the univocal and seamless expression of Christian orthodoxy did not long go unchallenged; in varying degrees, critics began to emphasize an element of inconsistency or contradiction in the play's attitude toward Faustus. In this development, the New Critical preoccupation with tension (resolved or unresolved) and ambivalence becomes conspicuous. Harry Levin interpreted the play as a tragedy of science without conscience, of knowledge as power that corrupts the soul; but he added that Marlowe hints at the arbitrariness of the Christian framework (with its grimly determinist Reformation theology) and "occasionally glances beyond it."[10] Robert Ornstein, who in 1955 had seen "no ambiguity or ambivalence" in the play (*MDF*, 171), concluded in

1968 that the play implicitly challenges the divine justice postulated by Christian theology, since the audience and a fallen angel pity what God cannot.[11]

More forceful versions of this response came from J. B. Steane (1964) and Wilbur Sanders (1968), each of whom found Marlowe failing to realize the elusive New Critical ideal of equilibrium, poise, or balance in the manipulation of opposed attitudes or beliefs. Sanders went so far as to claim that the play fails to realize its tragic potential, giving as his reasons that it is tied to Calvinist theology, which could not balance a sense of God's retributive justice with a vision of his sustaining love and mercy, and that it is caught between "the optimistic humanism propounded by the [Renaissance] apostles of perfectibility and an older mistrust of human aspirations to the divinity of knowledge." Marlowe's task was "to harmonise . . . two visions of the world, not by annihilating one in the interests of the other . . . but by [reaching] the deeper level where they were, if not reconciled, at least held in paradoxical synthesis." Had he achieved this "paradoxical harmony . . . we might have had a tragedy"; instead, Marlowe tried unsuccessfully to accommodate the underlying tragic dilemma to the old frontiers and boundaries of moralized experience and psychomachic conflict.[12] For Sanders, the irresolvable nature of the tragic paradox derived mainly from the presumed fact that Faustus does not simply choose a course of action that damns him but is predestined so to choose. F. P. Wilson noted that (by contrast with Spira's case of conscience, where the remorseful Protestant is convinced he is a reprobate), "there is nothing of predestination or reprobation in Marlowe's share of the play" and that he took his conception of the theme from his source, *The Damnable Life*: "Give none the blame but thine own self-will, thy proud and aspiring mind" (Wilson, 78). But Sanders interpreted the play as implicitly positing "a malignant universe . . . of irrational reprobation"; thus Faustus is not so much the victim of his own character as of Calvin's "appalling," "murderous and irresistible deity" (Sanders, 228).

Behind the interpretations of Steane and Sanders lies Una Ellis-Fermor's essay "The Equilibrium of Tragedy" (1945). This piece arguably constitutes the definitive application of New Critical poetics to the theory of tragedy. According to Ellis-Fermor, the best tragedy achieves an equilibrium in which a strict balance is preserved between two contrary readings of life. This occurs in Aeschylus, Sophocles, and Shakespeare, where "evident evil" is poised against "partially hidden and overruling good." (How balance is maintained when one force overrules the other is not explained.) The desired equilibrium, however, is not achieved in Marlowe's *Doctor Faustus*, where we find "a Satanic universe" that rests on an "implacable paradox," that of "man's innate fallibility" and "the infallibility demanded by inflexible law." Like his contemporary Fulke Greville (author of the tragedy *Mustapha*), Marlowe saw the "Wearisome condition of humanity, / Born under one law, to another bound." He did not explicitly affirm "the predestination of man to destruction," but the premise is implied in several passages.[13] This view of *Doctor Faustus*, in which a purported (but undoubtedly debatable) textual commitment to Calvinist reprobation is said to produce irresolvable contradiction and paradox, has had a widespread and lasting influence.

The most notable changes in recent criticism of *Doctor Faustus* have been effected by the new historicism and cultural materialism. These are twin forms of historical criticism, in that they share a common interest in the ideological pressures and political forces that lie behind the meaning patterns of the text. For such critics, the significance of the moral, psychological, philosophical, and religious problems raised by a text is ultimately political. Their primary concern is arguably less with the text itself than with its sociopolitical origins, less with its meaning than with the (political) meaning of its meanings. And the political invariably signifies a power struggle in which ideology functions as the instrument whereby a dominant minority can exercise control over a largely deluded majority. This perspective on culture, society, and history is basically Marxist. It is conspicuous in the interpretations of *Doctor Faustus* offered by the new historicist Stephen Greenblatt in *Renaissance Self-Fashioning* (1980) and by the cultural materialist Jonathan Dollimore in *Radical Tragedy* (1984). As a play that deals with an individual's revolt against omnipotent authority, *Doctor Faustus* would seem to invite interpretation as a vehicle of their shared worldview. The tacit assumption behind their initial approach to Faustus is that his rebellion has to be seen as justifiable, since all authority is to be equated with power, and all power with constricting domination.

For Greenblatt, all Marlowe's plays subvert the Renaissance belief that human identity is to a considerable extent self-constructed. In agreement with an axiom laid down by Michel Foucault (perhaps his chief theoretical mentor), he found that the human subject in Marlowe is shown to be remarkably unfree, and an ideological product of the relations of power in the society to which he belongs. Indeed, personal identity is seen to be no more than a theatrical invention achieved by constantly repeating the same kind of sustaining but goalless action.[14] Faustus's use of biblical quotations such as "Consummatum est," or "It is finished" (Christ's dying words, John 19.30), and the way in which his voluptuous pleasures turn out to be parodic versions of Holy Communion, illustrate the dependence of his identity on the culture he would reject and his failure to define himself in terms of a truly radical, materialistic worldview (213–14). The dependence of identity on repetitive action is apparent in his constant movement from thinking of the joys of heaven, through despairing of ever possessing them, to embracing magical power as a substitute (210). Many other critics would wish to explain these aspects of Faustus's behavior differently. They might observe that blasphemous parody was a traditional feature of witchcraft and diabolism, the devil being seen as "the ape of God" and devilry as a grotesque attempt to usurp divinity. They might also observe that since the Christian worldview, however severe, is accepted as truth for the purposes of the play, the idea that Faustus should define himself in relation to any other model of reality is irrelevant, and that Faustus's constant oscillation between hope, despair, and magical distractions simply reflects his tortured inability to cope with the situation into which he has projected himself.

Marxist critics invariably focus on the phenomenon of contradiction, since in their theory of historical change, that is the key to the inevitable collapse of feudal and capitalist systems and their supporting idealist ideologies. For this reason, Ellis-Fermor's 1945 reading of *Doctor Faustus* is recycled in Jonathan Dollimore's Marxist analysis of the play. The Calvinist emphasis on human sinfulness, he explains, constituted a "stress point in protestantism which plays like *Dr Faustus* (and *Mustapha*) exploit." Tossed between God and Lucifer, two tyrants "equally responsible for his final destruction," Faustus inhabits "a violently divided universe" whose very essence is "conflict and contradiction." The Calvinist doctrine of predestination (claimed Dollimore) was a doctrine of naked power, which contemporary tyrants exploited as part of an ideological mystification of their own power. Thus, the implicit questioning of divine power in *Doctor Faustus*—"indictment" of "an authoritarian discourse . . . through ironic allegiance"—anticipates a similar response to political authority in the overtly political tragedies of the Jacobean period and locates the play in a subversive movement that was to culminate in the revolution of 1642.[15] One problem with this interpretation is that all the verbal and dramatic irony of the play is directed not at divine power but—clearly and forcefully—at Faustus's delusions concerning his own power. Whether Faustus was predestined for damnation is an entirely open question. Furthermore, since Queen Elizabeth, head of the established church, angrily refused to allow the doctrine of reprobation to become part of the church's official teaching, it cannot be maintained that an antireprobationist stance would make the play politically subversive (see chapter 9).

Not all contemporary critics of *Doctor Faustus* are willing to take the risks that Greenblatt and Dollimore did in adjusting the text to a preconceived theory or ideology; the inductive habit of according full respect to all the text's verbal and nonverbal signs and making them the unmistakable basis for general positions is still in evidence.[16] But these are two challenging and influential critics whose arguments require careful attention. In reading them, the student will become conscious that in an age as preoccupied as ours with theory, the danger of transgressing the line between legitimate new insights and subtle or unsubtle misrepresentation is greater than it ever was in the age of romanticism.

A READING

4

Source, Design, Genre

The story of the man who sells his soul to the devil for some special favor existed in many forms in the Middle Ages; it has, however, become almost wholly identified with the name of Faust, a historical person who died in 1541. This Faust was a boastful charlatan who went about Germany calling himself "the prince of necromancers"; he was scorned by the learned, condemned by churchmen, and a source of wonder to the gullible. Numerous marvels were attributed to him during his lifetime and thereafter. In 1587 his legend bore profitable fruit in the enormously popular *Historia von D. Johann Fausten*, printed and possibly also written by Johann Spies. An English translation by one P.F., *The Historie of the Damnable Life and Deserved Death of Doctor John Faustus*, was published in 1592, but this is a reprint of an earlier edition of which no copy has survived. Marlowe's play is based on this translation.

The *Damnable Life* is an unsubtle, sensationalistic, and moralizing work, but Marlowe must have detected in its legendary subject a restless spiritual rebel with whom he could easily identify. The troublesome son of a poor man, Faust was sent by a rich uncle to the University of Wittenberg to study theology. He proved to be a student of exceptional brilliance and was duly awarded a doctorate in divinity; but he had no real interest in the queen of the sciences (as it was termed) and quickly threw away the Scriptures. He then "fell into such fantasies and deep cogitations that he was . . . called the Speculator" and gave himself up to the study of the "devilish arts" of necromancy and conjuration, at first secretly, but then openly, to the horror and wonderment of his contemporaries.[1]

The former scholarship youth from Canterbury who studied theology at Cambridge, who rejected a career in the church for one on the stage (an illusionist art long held by theologians to be allied to idolatry, magic, and devilry), and who quickly became notorious for his openly blasphemous and skeptical opinions could not but have seen a strange resemblance to himself in this figure. Indeed, the German author's repeated condemnation of Faust's irreligion and damnable "pride and high mind"—that sin for which "Lucifer is thrust and fallen out of heaven" (71)—was not at all unlike the kind of language directed at Marlowe by some of his shocked contemporaries. But, although Marlowe enters imaginatively into the spirit of the restless and proud speculator, articulating in richest poetry his longings for forbidden knowledge, power, and pleasure, and using him to blaspheme outrageously from the stage, no protagonist of Renaissance tragedy is subjected to such insistent and searchingly ironic questioning. Faustus's heroic self-conception is cruelly debunked, and the discrepancy between his expectations (far more extravagant than those ascribed to him in *The Damnable Life*) and his achievements is emphasized in such a way that it seems ludicrous as well as tragic. One might well be puzzled as to why Marlowe should treat the legendary speculator thus; he, more than any of his contemporaries, could have been expected to endow intellectual rebelliousness with a certain indestructible strength and dignity and at least protect it from belittlement. Perhaps Marlowe wanted to avoid the charge of self-glorification: much like James Joyce, who in his autobiographical novel *Stephen Hero* and its rewritten version, *A Portrait of the Artist as a Young Man*, heavily ironized the self-consciously heroic rebelliousness of his fictionalized self. Marlowe would also have been affected by his awareness of the censor's pen and of his own perilous relationship with the authorities. Perhaps, too, a part of him may have come to recognize an element of immaturity and posturing in his own outrageousness.

Arguably, however, *Doctor Faustus* is not so much a play about intellectual rebellion as about "mental suffering,"[2] about regret, fear, and despair, figured as the hero's intermittent but intense moments of contact with reality during a lifetime of delusion and illusion. Of the 63 chapters in *The Damnable Life*, about 5 (scattered here and there) deal with Faustus's regrets and his abortive attempts to repent and return to God. In the play, this element in the original is foregrounded. It competes in power, if not in space, with the element of rebellion and showmanship, and culminates in the magnificent closing scene, where Marlowe is at his very greatest as a poetic dramatist.

The Damnable Life is a loose episodic narrative rather roughly divided into three parts. The first part (chapters 1–17, comprising 25 percent of the whole) deals with Faustus's early years, his theological studies, his introduction to necromancy, his signing the pact with the devil, and his questioning of Mephistophiles about the secrets of hell and matters astronomical. The second part (chapters 16–28, or 35 percent of the whole) deals exclusively with Faust's desire to know more about the spiritual and the physical world, a desire that prompts visionary, celestial, and terrestial travels. The third part (chapters 29–63, or 40 percent of the whole) focuses more on power and pleasure than on knowledge; it tells of Faustus's magical performances in the courts of German princes, of his various pranks or "merry conceits," of his carousals with his friends and his coupling (in his last year) with Helen of Troy, and finally with his "miserable and lamentable end" (201).

Marlowe's play follows the general outline of this plotless narrative and remains quite close to it in the content and detail of certain scenes. But the playwright's interpretative emphases, his theatrical sense, and his need to impose some kind of unity on the episodic structure dictate much change in the way of contraction, expansion, and addition. Faustus's signing of the pact, for example, comes much later than in the original (one-third of the way from the start as opposed to one-twentieth), Marlowe being greatly concerned with the psychological process (involving desire, excitement, anxiety, fear, and inner conflict) that precedes and attends it and with making it stand out as a momentous event, a "proud audacious deed" with terrible consequences. The scene in which Mephastophilis[3] and Faustus invisibly attend and violently disrupt the pope's feast during their travels through Italy is given far more prominence than in the original. The action functions as an audacious deed of climactic importance and marks the height of Faustus's worldly power—the nearest he comes to fulfilling his promise to become "great emperor of the world" (3.105).

In contrast, the proportion of magical tricks and pranks offered in the third part of The Damnable Life is greatly reduced, and the attention given to Faustus's union with Helen and his fearful end (as a final, arresting conjunction of illusion and reality, pleasure and retribution) is correspondingly increased. The figures of the Good Angel, the Evil Angel, and the conjurers Cornelius and Valdes are additions that function as part of Marlowe's attention to the drama of temptation and spiritual conflict. Scenes involving witty and clownish servants are also inserted, giving that mixture of the comic and the tragic that was condemned during the Renaissance by the classically minded but required in the popular theater and well established in the native dramatic tradition from medieval times. Like The Damnable Life, however, the play remains very much a narrative about only two characters, the magician and his familiar spirit.

The original texts of the play have no act or scene divisions. The only marking points are the five choruses, which provide narrative summary and a sense of classical gravity and elevation (the first and last being prologue and epilogue). The second chorus introduces that section of the play that deals with Faustus's Grand Tour of the heavens and the earth to "know the secrets of astronomy" and to "prove cosmography" (chor.2.2,7). The third chorus heralds his return to Germany and his exhibitions of magical power to his mighty and lowly compatriots. The fourth marks off the final phase: the escapist carousals, the Old Man's appeal for repentance, the struggle between hope and despair, union with Helen, and seizure by the devils.

The second and third choruses coincide exactly with the divisions between the second and third sections of The Damnable Life. It might seem therefore that with the addition of the fourth chorus, Marlowe had in mind a four-act play—like Thomas Kyd's *The Spanish Tragedy* (c. 1585–90)—based on a simple expansion of the original three-part structure (part three being split near the end). But this would mean that the first act takes up half the play. It might more plausibly be argued that there is a classical five-act division, the beginning of the second act being marked by Faustus's soliloquy "Now Faustus, must thou needs be damned . . . ?" (Gill, 5.1ff.), which falls midway between the first and second choruses and introduces the long, crucially important scene— constituting, in this hypothesis, Act II—where Faustus signs the deed for Mephastophilis and meets his new master, Lucifer.[4] Seen thus, the play reveals a structure where the first act deals with the hero's rebellious desires, the second act with his fatal choice, the third and fourth with his exercise of magical powers abroad and at home, and the fifth with inescapable reality and retribution.

The five-act division remains conjectural. There are other unmistakable strategies by which Marlowe imposes significant unity on his episodic narrative, and these warrant much more attention. There is first of all the rise-and-fall pattern. This is explicitly signaled in the imagery and diction of the first and second choruses and structurally reflected in the placement of Faustus's aerial flight and triumph over the pope—supreme earthly potentate—at the approximate center of the play (immediately after chorus 2). The final chorus (i.e., the epilogue) explicitly marks the completion of a trajectory that takes Faustus from "parents base of stock" (chor.1.11) to "Jove's high firmament" (chor.2.3) and princely courts, and then downward to bottomless depths:

> Faustus is gone! Regard his hellish fall,
> Whose fiendful fortune may exhort the wise
> Only to wonder at unlawful things;
> Whose deepness doth entice such forward wits
> To practice more than heavenly power permits. (chor.5.4–8)

Rising too high and then falling was the paradigm structure for tragedy in the Middle Ages and the Renaissance, and it was closely associated, as here, with the image of Fortune's wheel.[5]

Marlowe's use of archetypal symbols in characterizing Faustus serves not only to magnify and universalize his tragedy but also to lend imaginative unity to the play. From the outset, Faustus is associated with archetypal representatives of hubristic ascent and tragic fall: with Icarus, the reckless and ambitious youth of classical myth who ignored his father Daedalus's warning not to fly too near the sun ("his waxen wings did mount above his reach, / And melting heavens conspired his overthrow" (chor.1.21–22); with Lucifer (Satan's name before his fall), whom "God threw . . . from the face of heaven" because of his "aspiring pride and insolence" (3.68–69; see also 5.155); and with Adam, who disobeyed God's command not to eat from the Tree of the Knowledge of Good and Evil, thus causing that primal fall that in Christian theology accounts for all the miseries of the human condition.[6] As a source of unity, the Adamic parallel is perhaps the most valuable of these archetypal symbols, since it gives rise to a network of imagistic and verbal motifs that permeate the whole play. According to the Book of Genesis, the forbidden fruit was both good to taste and "pleasant to the eyes." The serpent told Eve that if she and Adam ate it their eyes would be opened and they would be as gods, knowing good and evil. When they ate, "the eyes of them both were opened"—but opened to their own sinfulness and God's anger (Gen. 3.4–7). All this is reflected in Faustus's insistent desire to become godlike, in the many literal and figurative references to gluttonous eating and drinking, and in an ocular motif on which numerous variations are played. Faustus's act of signing the deed in which he barters his soul for forbidden power, knowledge, and pleasure is equivalent to Adam and Eve's eating the apple, and it, too, becomes a recurrent motif: a covert pun on the word *deed* ensures that all Faustus's "proud audacious deeds" (chor.1.5) are reminders of the spiritual implications and fatal consequences of his "deed of gift." Wordplay is also used to multiply instances of the ocular motif.

The unifying principle at work in these symbols and images is that of analogy. As in medieval and Renaissance drama and narrative generally, analogy is a major source of unity at the structural as well as the verbal level in *Doctor Faustus*. This is most apparent in the relationship between the comic subplot scenes and the central tragic action. The scenes with Wagner and the scholars (scene 2), Wagner and the Clown (scene 4), and Robin, Rafe, and the Vintner (scenes 6, 8) could be removed from the play without rendering the tragic action any the less intelligible, but they contain precise, unspoken parallels between the antics of the comic characters and the folly of the tragic hero. There is a sense in which all tragic characters are fools, blind to the nature of reality, impetuous in a way that distinguishes them from the cautious and prudent majority. But *The Damnable Life* was a hybrid mixture of two kinds of book, a biography of a legendary wonderworker (whether magician or saint) and a collection of merry tales and pranks,[7] so that Faustus came to Marlowe as an incongruous mixture of superman and trickster. Thus, some of the scenes in which Faustus exhibits his magical powers (as when he fools Pope Adrian or the Horse-Courser) are no less undignified and silly than those involving the "low" characters.

In modern times, actors playing Faustus have always had the greatest difficulty integrating the two sides of his character (or the two Faustuses), and it has to be admitted that for most viewers and readers the play is marred by a profound unevenness that seems to stem from the protagonist's originally and intractably split persona. But here, too, analogy contributes in considerable measure to a resolution of the problem that faced the playwright. The pranks that Faustus plays on others are all shaped and phrased so as to provide an ironic reflection of his own spiritual predicament. Indeed, this is also the case in those situations where his demonstrations of supernatural powers are conducted in an atmosphere of becoming gravity. Through analogy, the episodic always becomes part of the underlying spiritual plot.

The analogies are always ironic, in the sense that they remind the audience of a reality to which the hero is blind or which he is trying to forget. Irony is one of the most valuable and characteristic devices of the dramatist, especially the tragic dramatist.[8] It is a silent mode of commentary in a medium where economy is of the utmost importance. It acts as the shadow or voice of fate. It generates suspense and imaginative involvement and keeps spectators in that state of mind where they long to warn the character on the stage before them of what lies ahead. And of course irony effects unity by linking the present to the future and to the past. The forms of irony in *Doctor Faustus* are rich and various; they might be classified as verbal (puns and ambiguities), situational, proleptic or prospective, retrospective, inversive (reality upside-down), and analogical.

The theme of sin, repentance, and redemption or damnation, the combination of the grave and the comic-grotesque, the figures of the Good and the Bad Angels (externalizing the protagonist's spiritual conflict), and the contrary roles of the corrupting magicians Cornelius and Valdes, on the one hand, and the spiritually supportive Old Man, on the other, all link *Doctor Faustus* with the late medieval tradition of the morality play. But elements of the morality play survived in most Renaissance tragedies, and it can hardly be denied that *Doctor Faustus* is—and was intended to be—a tragedy rather than a morality play. Doubts as to whether *Doctor Faustus* can be properly called a tragedy have a variety of causes and have been expressed in different ways. Those who employ the term *tragedy* more as a badge of distinction than as a descriptive term, who will not entertain the concept of a flawed masterpiece and are convinced that distinguished literary art always projects an identifiable balance of contradictory value systems or worldviews, necessarily see *Doctor Faustus* as a play that fails to rise above the contradictions and incongruities generated by its morality inheritance. To this, we must respond that the theory of equilibrium is questionable, not least because critics who hold to it are often in complete disagreement as to whether a particular text achieves the required equilibrium or not.

More important perhaps is the claim that the play fails to meet the requirements of tragedy because the protagonist lacks true heroic quality: he may tower above the rest of humanity at the start because of the extravagance of his desires and the recklessness of his choice, but he quickly displays all the weakness, foolishness, and timidity of the Everyman figure that he is, and he dies in sheer terror, without a trace of Stoic dignity or unrepentant defiance. This argument often comes backward into critical discussion through the determination of the critic to ignore all that is weak and petty in Faustus's character and, sidestepping the numerous ironies, to take him on his own terms as an exemplar of resolution and "manly fortitude" (386). An example is when R. B. Sewall stated that at death "he goes out no craven sinner, but violently, speaking the rage and despair of all mankind,"[9] or when Nicholas Brooke claimed that he actually chooses hell and rejects heaven as unworthy of him.

The notion that the tragic hero must be the epitome of manliness is class-based (aristocratic) and military; it is a theory derived from a culture which determined that epics (heroic poems) and tragedies could only be about the doings and sufferings of "great men," noble individuals in both the social and the characterological sense. Thanks in no small measure to the morality tradition, *Doctor Faustus* proves triumphantly that the sufferings of a man very like the rest of us (and perhaps even sillier and weaker than many of us would like to think of ourselves as) can engage us emotionally and intellectually at the deepest level.

Our notion of what is tragic need not be dependent on the idea of heroic greatness in the sense implied above. It should be determined rather by the play's capacity to excite pity, fear, wonder, and bewilderment at the spectacle of human suffering, and to set us pondering on the problematic relationship between justice and injustice or between the intelligible and the incomprehensible in the price men have to pay for their fatal errors and misdeeds. *Doctor Faustus* has such a capacity, not least because it is dominated throughout by the imagined reality of hell. We may not believe in hell and may even consider it to be one of the most ghastly creations of the human mind, but we can easily accept it in this play as suffering, loss, and terrible consequence rendered absolute.

5

Divinity and Magic

In the very year that Marlowe first astounded London audiences with *Tamburlaine the Great* (1587), Reginald Scot, a fellow Kentish man, published his *Discoverie of Witchcraft*. This work was prompted by the trial of the so-called witches of St. Osyths, near Chelmsford (Essex), in which 16 of the accused women were found guilty and 13 executed. Himself a lawyer and magistrate, Scot had assisted at the witchcraft trial of Margaret Symons at the Rochester assizes in Kent in 1581; having cross-examined the accused, he dismissed the case against her. His attitude toward witchcraft was one of almost total skepticism, and in the *Discoverie* he reduced the whole mythology of the subject—the miracles and the terrible crimes alike—to the delusions induced in old women by melancholy and the "fantasticall confessions" extracted from them under torture by superstitious and credulous judges. "Witchcraft and inchantment is the cloke of ignorance," declared Scot.[1]

However, Scot's humane and rational position was untypical. The learned King James VI of Scotland wrote his *Daemonologie* to controvert Scot's skeptical views, and when he became James I of England, he ordered that all existing copies of the *Discoverie* be burnt. The witch craze that began in the late Middle Ages in Western Europe reached its climax in the sixteenth century, thanks as much to pious and scholarly men as to the fears and fantasies of the uneducated. It begot a reign of terror and cruelty that remains a major blot on the history of Christianity. We can surmise with almost complete certainty that Marlowe's attitude toward witchcraft would have been much the same as Scot's. It was, however, as a professional playwright with an eye to success in the popular theater, and not as a rationalist, that he dramatized *The Damnable Life*. Although he was obviously attracted to the legend as a parable on the desire to transcend human limitations, on the misery of a man trapped in the consequences of a rash deed, and on the characteristically Reformation experience of doubt and despair, the story's sensational supernaturalism was its major attraction to the theatergoing public and had to be left intact.

Witchcraft, or black magic, is of pre-Christian and indeed of prehistoric origin. It implies the exercise of supernatural powers—always defined in Christian times as demonic—for wicked purposes. In the early Christian period it was identified by the fathers of the church with paganism or idolatry, as it had been by the authors of the Old Testament.[2] The miraculous powers imputed to the old gods by their followers were not dismissed out of hand but were treated either as devilishly inspired fictions or as illusions and marvels worked by means of magic and the assistance of demons.[3] Since the Greeks had identified their anthropomorphic divinities with the stars, which were believed to influence earthly affairs for good and ill, astrology was closely associated with black magic in Christian teaching.

In contrast, the New Testament provided a favorable view of astrology in the figures of the Wise Men, or Magi (magicians, astrologers), who, by reading the stars, came to worship the infant Christ. Moreover, astrology was not firmly distinguished from astronomy until the seventeenth century. So Christian doctrine accepted the pre-Christian distinction between white and black magic, although it tended to suggest that the distinction was very unstable. Black magic included all forms of astrological divination or of witchcraft that involved the invocation of demons.[4] White magic was essentially natural science, proceeding from an attempt to harness the occult powers of nature for legitimate ends; it included attempts to discover how stellar influence would affect the weather, the fate of nations, or the health of the individual. Natural or white magic in various forms flourished during the Renaissance and, under the influence of Neoplatonism, acquired a distinctly mystical character. It was viewed by men like Ficino, Paracelsus, Cornelius Agrippa, and John Dee as a means of acquiring access to the divine through nature. Endowed with grace, the wise man "could seek out those substances which correspond to the celestial bodies and therefore ultimately the Creator."[5] But the mystically minded scientist of the Renaissance who allowed himself to be called a magician put himself in grave danger, since the suspicion of devilry was still attached to all forms of magic.[6] Agrippa was branded as a black magician by influential demonologists such as Jean Bodin and Martin del Rio. (Marlowe's play seems to concur with this view when Faustus enthuses about Agrippa and "infernal spirits" in one and the same sentence [1.117].) Dee, who was Queen Elizabeth's personal astrologer and a distinguished mathematician, was similarly condemned and ended his life in poverty and disgrace.[7]

Many perhaps would have looked on Agrippa and Dee as mystical scientists whose lofty conception of their art was gradually corrupted. They would have been seen as white magicians who by degrees slipped into demonism after having failed in their attempts to reach the divine through nature's occult powers. Marlowe's Faustus (like Spies's) cannot be seen in this light, although some critics have been inclined to think so. When Faustus first considers magic, it is to "negromantic books" (1.50) and the demonic invocations of "the black art" (9.2) that he turns.[8] His subsequent career has most of the standard ingredients of the witch's life as described in priestly sixteenth-century books on the subject: renunciation of the faith or certain of its dogmas, the demonic pact, a declared willingness to sacrifice babies to the devil, aerial transportation, invisibility, bodily transformation, lustfulness and copulation with a demon (a succubus), prevention by demons from weeping and repenting.[9]

Nevertheless, Faustus is unquestionably an intellectual with a passion for knowledge, and it is that which raises him far above the level of the vulgar witch as characterized in the demonological manuals. As the opening soliloquy emblematically indicates, he has reached

a crossroads in his life after having achieved preeminence in philosophy, medicine, law, and divinity. Dissatisfied with these, he turns to
necromancy with thoughts that stretch "as far as doth the mind of
man" (1.61). He hopes that the spirits will read him "strange philosophy" and "resolve . . . all ambiguities" (1.80, 86). Having signed the
deed, he harries Mephastophilis with questions about the spirit world
and "divine astrology" (5.210). Soon, too, his aerial and terrestial journeys act out a boundless desire for the kinds of knowledge that the age
of Galileo and Columbus could not but have approved. Faustus also
has plans to use his newfound powers in a material manner that
Marlowe's audience would have deemed truly heroic: he would protect his country with a wall of brass (1.88, 93) and drive the Spanish
governor-general, the Prince of Parma, out of the Netherlands—to the
benefit not only of the Netherlanders but also of the English, since
Parma was to have assisted the Armada of 1588.

It cannot, however, be said that Faustus ever sought knowledge
either for its own sake or for the ends approved by Christianity, or
that the uses to which he intends to put his necromantic books and his
spirits are primarily or substantially altruistic. Faustus approaches
magic in a spirit of wild and dizzy excitement about all its possible
uses, with a mind, as it were, out of all control as it contemplates a
world in which he will have the freedom to do anything and everything he can possibly imagine. There is a kind of boyish abandon—
"'Tis magic, magic that hath ravished me" (1.110)—in his speculations
that makes the Icarian analogy singularly apt.

The chief satisfaction that the study of philosophy, medicine,
law, and theology has given Faustus is his ability to "gravel" or con-
found his academic peers and boost his own "flowering pride." (He
speaks of *their* pride in these lines [1.141–43], but it is his own pride
that we are conscious of.) He abandons these studies because they do
not finally assuage his feelings of inadequacy as an individual and a
human being. Law is a "petty," "paltry" profession that "fits a merce-
nary drudge, / Who aims at nothing but external trash, / Too servile
and illiberal for me" (30–36); logic affords "no greater miracle" than
to dispute well (37); medicine leaves him unable to make a man live
eternally; divinity reminds him of sin and death. Faustus's pride

demands nothing less than divine power, if only for a limited period: "A sound magician is a mighty god. / Here Faustus, try thy brains to gain a deity" (62–63). And for him, being godlike means escape from a sense of subservience that is both social and ontological; his overriding desire is to deliver commands that will all be instantly obeyed. "All things that move within the quiet poles shall be at my command," he tells himself (85–86). He expects to "Be . . . on earth as Jove is in the sky, / Lord and commander" of elemental nature (76–77) and of all creatures. His spirits will be "servile" and "perform what desperate enterprise I will" (110, 126). In response to his command, even "great Mephastophilis" will be "full of obedience and humility" (3.31, 34; cf. 3.98). Faustus himself will "reign sole king" when the Spanish have been driven out (1.94). In fact, he "will be great emperor of the world" and other rulers will all be subservient and "contributory" to him, just as they were to the conquering hero of *Tamburlaine the Great*: "The emperor shall not live but by my leave, / Nor any potentate in Germany" (3.110–12).

Faustus's folly in bartering his soul with the hope of achieving all this seems totally at odds with the great intellect with which he is credited at the outset. We are to understand, presumably, that his boundless pride and excitable imagination—the sheer intensity of his desire to assert himself and escape from all human limitations—bring about his downfall by playing tricks with that intellect. Faustus "tries his brains" to justify a course of action that a less imaginative and less ambitious person would rightly judge to be perilous in the extreme. Pointers to this conception of his fall are given in his opening soliloquy, a speech that obviously records in condensed and stylized form a prolonged mental debate. He begins the soliloquy with the decision to "settle" his studies, to "sound the depth" of whatever subject he will "profess" (follow, teach), and to examine the "end" or purpose of every branch of study. In the next sentence, he decides to abandon the study of logic on the ground that he has achieved its end, which is to argue well. But we quickly sense that Faustus is very unsettled in his mind, that he does not sound the depth of his subjects, does not reason logically, and that he has forgotten the ends of all study as defined by the subject in which he has taken his doctorate—that is, to bring humans to a better understanding of God's creation, of their own place in it, and of God's nature.

Of especial significance is the way in which Faustus argues for abandoning theology and the Scriptures. On the basis of two biblical quotations, one from Romans 6.23 ("The reward of sin is death"), and the other from 1 John 1.8 ("If we say we have no sin, we deceive ourselves"), he constructs a syllogism (a standard form of logical argument) proving that Christian doctrine is grimly fatalistic and therefore to be rejected: "Why then belike we must sin and so consequently die . . . an everlasting death" (40–46). As has often been noted (but not by critics in the romantic tradition), Marlowe has subtly disqualified this argument by allowing Faustus to ignore the following verse in each of the two epistles, which emphasizes God's forgiveness and his "gift of . . . eternal life" (Rom. 6.24). (Adam's sin and Christ's "ransoming blood" is the pervasive theme of Paul's epistle.) Faustus's flippantly dismissive and punning "Divinity, adieu!" (48) confirms the impression of a mind that is willfully skimming over the surface of things profound.

Willful blindness or self-deception was said by theologians to be a characteristic of many sinners; whereas it is lightly suggested in this opening soliloquy, it is boldly dramatized in Faustus's first encounter with Mephastophilis. This is one of the two most brilliant and moving scenes in the whole play. In stark contrast to the seductively reassuring performance of the conjurers Cornelius and Valdes in the previous scene and to the behavior of the stereotypical tempting demon, Mephastophilis's conduct here is, in effect, that of a resolutely honest and deeply concerned friend. He quickly seeks to disabuse Faustus of his delighted belief that his conjurations give him real power over spirits and that he is heroically unique. Mephastophilis explains carefully—even pedantically—that he came of his own accord when Faustus conjured him, and may do no more for him than Lucifer permits. He adds that what he will do for Faustus he would do for anyone who will deny God and barter "his glorious soul" (3.41–55). But these revelations have no effect on Faustus's buoyant mood. He proceeds to question Mephastophilis lightly about his master Lucifer (as if *he* were any ordinary prince) and is reminded in heavily accented terms that Lucifer was once "most dearly loved of God" but was thrown from heaven because of his "aspiring pride and insolence" (3.65–69).

Unaffected by the pointed analogy, Faustus proceeds to question Mephastophilis about himself and seeks, in his old disputatious manner, to catch him in logical contradiction: if it is true that he is in hell, "how comes it then that thou art out of hell?" To which comes this extraordinary reply:

> Why this is hell, nor am I out of it.
> Thinkst thou that I, who saw the face of God,
> And tasted the eternal joys of heaven,
> Am not tormented with ten thousand hells
> In being deprived of everlasting bliss!
> O Faustus, leave these frivolous demands,
> Which strike a terror to my fainting soul. (3.77–83)

In return for this cry of anguish, horror, and compassion, the "melancholy demon" (as Victorian critics liked to call him) is taunted for his emotionalism and mockingly advised to learn from Faustus "manly fortitude" and the ability to scorn those joys he will never possess (3.84–87).

It is a mistake to look for complete consistency of characterization in Renaissance drama. The playwrights of this period would happily renounce such consistency for the sake of vivid local effect, reinforcement of a governing theme, or illumination of another character. Marlowe presents us here with an entirely original kind of devil, but that is not at all his intention; in fact, Mephastophilis's behavior at this point is totally at variance with both his intentions and his conduct as shown later. He has been presented at the start as devastatingly truthful and urgently helpful simply in order to emphasize the staggering extent of Faustus's blindness to reality and the fact that he is willfully choosing his own destiny. Once Faustus has reached the point of signing the deed, Mephastophilis becomes, and remains thereafter, the conventional "familiar": deceiving and seductive, wholly intent on ensuring the damnation of his gullible "master." This contrast between Mephastophilis's earlier and later conduct contributes to the impressively effective contrast in audience response to the earlier and the later Faustus: at first critical and detached, but later engaged and profoundly sympathetic. It is to this contrast perhaps that those in search of a tragic equilibrium should have looked, for it is one in which we can see a perfect balance of the basic tragic emotions defined by Aristotle: fear (detaching us from the proud, erring hero as a dangerous example) and pity (drawing us to him as a humbled and disillusioned victim of our common humanity and the impulses that ensnare us).

"Full of obedience and humility" was how Faustus saw Mephastophilis at first. The phrase describes no seducing familiar but the ideal Christian, who seeks to achieve his or her divinely ordained end, and also Adam and Eve before the serpent entered the garden. The Fall, prompted by a desire to become godlike, was caused by pride and disobedience, but sensuality was involved, too—Adam's desire for Eve, and her's for the apple that was good to taste and pleasant to the eye. Thus, in *Doctor Faustus* the Adamic analogy to Faustus's magical career is insisted on throughout in numerous literal and metaphorical references to gluttony and lust. Summarizing his career, the Prologue tells how, as a divine, Faustus is "glutted with learning's golden gifts" and thereafter "surfeits upon cursed necromancy: / Nothing so sweet as magic is to him" (chor.1.24–26). When the Evil Angel assures him he will be a Jove-like commander of the elements, he proclaims himself "glutted with conceit of this" (1.78). After being entertained by Lucifer with a pageant of the Seven Deadly Sins (including Gluttony and Lechery), he exclaims: "O this feeds my soul" (5.336). The word *cheer* is synonymous with *feed* when he responds with comparable enthusiasm to Cornelius's talk about "the miracles that magic will perform" for him: "O this cheers my soul!" (1.136, 149). According to Mephastophilis, the pope and his cardinals have reduced "St. Peter's holy feast" to "belly cheer," that being (in theological terminology) their "summum bonum" or supreme good (7.49, 51). He and Faustus make a shambles of the feast, turning themselves invisible and snatching the pope's wine and food as he reaches for them in vain. But Faustus's own life has become something of a riotous feast, and the way in which he marks its approaching end is characteristic. Says his servant Wagner:

> I think my master means to die shortly,
> For he hath given to me all his goods!
> And yet methinks, if that death were near,
> He would not banquet, and carouse, and swill,
> Amongst the students, as even now he doth,
> Who are at supper with such belly-cheer
> As Wagner ne'er beheld in all his life.
> See where they come: belike the feast is ended. (chor.4)

"The feast"—Faustus's hedonistic life as a magician—is not ended until he beholds in anguish "where Christ's blood streams in the firmament" (a kind of endless eucharistic wine) and longs in vain for one half-drop to save his soul from endless loss and torment (13.72–73). Like so much else in the last two scenes, the word *ended* brings us back in ironic circularity to the beginning, where Faustus's hungry desires blinded him to the end or purpose of all knowledge and to the nature of his own end.

In the "surfeit of deadly sin" (13.11) that Faustus himself finally confesses to, lust is not referred to quite so often as gluttony, but it figures promptly and conspicuously and it occasions, in the penultimate scene, the tragedy's most rhapsodic and memorable speech. The lust theme occurs not simply because of its expansion of the sensuality element in the archetypal Fall but also, and more important, because of its special association with witchcraft. According to the *Malleus Maleficarum*, the most influential and authoritative treatise in the vast body of literature on the subject, "all witchcraft comes from carnal lust" (47). This conviction is abundantly evident in the obsessive preoccupation in all this literature with the alleged nocturnal orgies of the witches and, above all, with their copulations with the devil—"Succubus to a man . . . Incubus to a woman" (*Malleus*, 26).

The witchcraft-lust equation has its origins in the perceived link between witchcraft and paganism (witches were universally held to worship and ride the air nightly with the goddess Diana)[10] and, beyond that, in the biblical and patristic identification of idolatry with lust. Polytheism was conceived as a form of spiritual adultery (an adulteration of true divinity) as well as an unfailing source of sexual impurity. The fathers of the church saw the festivities and fables of the heathen deities as having a treacherous, sensual glamour, a spirit of passionate orgiastic abandon, and they used all their polemical and persuasive skills to prove that the erotic allure of the old religions was part of the devil's characteristic strategy of attempting to win the faithful away from the worship of the true God and back to idolatry (i.e., devil worship).[11] It is because of this established and familiar theological argument that the function of classical mythology in *Doctor Faustus* differs from that in Marlowe's other plays. Like magic, mythology is conceived here as pseudodivinity. It does not serve the neutral and typically Renaissance purposes of aesthetic intensification and metaphoric extension. It has a dramatic role and, along with magic and astrology, acts as the "heavenly" illusion that lures Faustus into hell. As soon as Faustus rejects true divinity, the old gods—planetary and otherwise—invade his consciousness with theological inevitability: he will, say his tempting accomplices, the magicians Valdes and Cornelius, be "on earth as Jove is in the sky" (1.76), more famous even than Apollo, god of "the Delphian oracle" (1.143). It is "longing to view Orion's drizzling look" (3.2) that he begins his incantations. Through these incantations he is quickly identified with Lucifer (3.61–73), who is both a classical stellar divinity and a Christian demon. Later, according to the B text, he will "play Diana" (B.85) and reenact her famous punishment of Actaeon when he puts horns on the foolish knight Benvolio. But the climax of his mythological fantasies is, of course, his union with a succubus in the form of Helen of Troy—not a major goddess, but of divine extraction and the most famous symbol of classical eroticism.

The erotic theme begins early in the tragedy. Among the satisfactions that Valdes and Cornelius promise Faustus if he becomes a magician are spirits or succubi who will come like "unwedded maids, / Shadowing more beauty in their airy brows / Than in the white breasts of the Queen of Love"—Venus herself. Accordingly, when he decides to conjure the devils, he chooses a "lusty grove" where he will "have these joys in full possession" (1.127–29, 151–52). Before signing the deed, he asks Mephastophilis to be allowed to "live in all voluptuousness" (3.93). Shortly after Faustus signs it, he suddenly grows tired of quizzing Mephastophilis about hell and says, "But leaving off this, let me have a wife, the fairest maid in Germany, for I am wanton and lascivious" (5.139–41). Lawful love, however, the sacrament of marriage and a source of grace, is not permitted by the devils, so instead of a wife he is jokingly offered what a stage direction calls "a Devil dressed like a woman, with fireworks" (5.145)—a "hot whore" (147) indeed!—and then promised more attractive things:

> I'll cull thee out the fairest courtesans
> And bring them every morning to thy bed:
> She whom thine eye shall like, thy heart shall have,
> Be she as chaste as was Penelope,
> As wise as Saba, or as beautiful
> As was bright Lucifer before his fall. (5.150–55)

These two perspectives on the desired female—the perfect beauty and the fiery devil—coalesce at the end in the image of the legendary woman whose great beauty, the text reminds us (12.14, 19, 83, 96–97), not only enchanted Paris but brought the flames of destruction to Troy and its inhabitants.

Although this "Helen" signifies sin and flames and final damnation, she is also the projection of an aesthetic sense that ennobles sexual desire and turns Faustus's rapturous approach to his succubus into something quite unlike the disgusting copulations envisaged by the demonologists. The demonic Helen is an exquisite, fatal dream worthy of high tragedy. Although the circumstances and the verbal texture of Faustus's rhapsody encase it in irony from start to finish, the speech contributes enormously to that crucial shift of audience response in the last scenes from fearful and critical detachment to compassionate and even admiring identification. For the moment, we are all—if we respond to the magical poetry—complicit with paganism here:

Was this the face that launched a thousand ships,
And burnt the topless towers of Ilium?
Sweet Helen, make me immortal with a kiss:
Her lips suck forth my soul, see where it flies!
Come, Helen, come, give me my soul again.
Here will I dwell, for heaven is in these lips,
And all is dross that is not Helena! . . .
O thou art fairer than the evening air,
Clad in the beauty of a thousand stars,
Brighter art thou than flaming Jupiter
When he appeared to hapless Semele;
More lovely than the monarch of the sky
In wanton Arethusa's azured arms;
And none but thou shalt be my paramour. (12.81–100)

One very obvious aspect of this tragedy that never seems to be considered of any critical significance is the fact that Faustus is not simply a learned Christian who turns to black magic but a distinguished theologian, or "divine," who does so. This fact has some bearing on the subtle meanings and ironic effects of the play as well as on its relationship to Renaissance tragedy in general. As Marlowe handles it, the given fact has an insidious logic to it, for Faustus proceeds from the study of divinity to an attempt to participate in it: "Try thy brains to gain a deity" (1.63). Rather, Faustus proceeds from one school of divinity, based on "Jerome's Bible," to another, based on the "metaphysics of magicians" and "necromantic books" that are "heavenly" (38, 49–50). The correspondence between the two professions as located in words like *heavenly*, *metaphysics*, and *divine* introduces a comprehensive instance of the substance-shadow antithesis that pervades the play (and of which I shall have more to say later). More obviously, Faustus's status as a distinguished theologian adds a special touch of extremity to the nature of his tragic conduct, much like Lucifer's original position as the brightest and best, "most dearly loved of God" (3.65). Faustus becomes, in a sense, his own antithesis, and in that respect the pattern of his development is typical of Renaissance tragic tradition. The theologian who becomes a devil worshiper can be compared, for example, to the cultured and humane judge of *The*

Spanish Tragedy who is transformed into a ruthless Machiavellian assassin or to the gentle, reflective idealist of *Julius Caesar* who slaughters his friend and dips his hands in his blood before running through the streets crying, "Peace, freedom, and liberty!" The antithetical nature of the hero's transformation to be found in so many Renaissance tragedies reflects a conviction, which the playwrights shared with the critical theorists of the time, that tragedy should excite not only fear and commiseration but also wonder and amazement.[12]

6

Inversion

In the Christian perspective, witchcraft was devilry masquerading as divinity, fraudulent omnipotence as true omnipotence, shadow as substance, black as white. Thus, the world of black magic is a world upside down, its governing principle being that of inversion.

The inversion principle is also dictated by the rebellious, mocking spirit of the witch, directed mainly at those things that are held most sacred by the rejected spiritual order. The devils, says the *Malleus Maleficarum*, "nearly always instruct witches to make their instruments of witchcraft by means of the Sacraments or sacramental things of the Church, or some holy thing consecrated of God . . . so that they the more deeply offend God their Creator" (115–16). More important to an understanding of inversion in the Christian view of witchcraft is the spirit of emulation, imitation, and consequent delusion. The devil presents himself to the magician as a god, demands divine homage, and even encourages his worshiper to think of himself as divine. Faustus was by no means the first of his kind to claim that "a sound magician is a mighty god" (1.62; see Lea, 119). Thus, although mocking inversion in *Doctor Faustus* is often deliberate on the part of the protagonist, a kind of reckless, exuberant blasphemy, more often and finally, it operates at his own expense, exposing him as the victim of a wholly false vision of reality, so that, in the apt phrasing of the B text, his end is to "tumble in confusion" (B.107), where "confusion" signifies both "intellectual disorder" and "perdition."

The strain of hectic or grim comedy which is never far from this process of essentially tragic confusion is due not only to established notions of devil and witch as "the ape of God" but in some measure also to the influence of the Saturnalian tradition of carnival festivity. In the medieval Christmastide celebrations known as the Feast of Fools and the Boy Bishop, inversion was the main structuring principle.[1] In the first, the despised minor clergy attached to a cathedral elected from the lowliest in their own ranks a "bishop," "archbishop," "pope," or "king"; then, within the cathedral itself, they would don monstrous masks and engage in an elaborate and noisy burlesque of those sacred ceremonies that they performed with due seriousness throughout the year. In the second form of revelry, Boy Bishop, the choirboys and servers at the cathedrals followed the same procedure, though in less riotous fashion.

These annual explosions of wild irreverence often went to astonishing extremes, provoking fierce ecclesiastical denunciation and sharp reminders that they had their origin in pagan worship and were "hateful to God and delightful to the demons."[2] The authors of the *Malleus* connected them with both idolatry and the rites of witchcraft (see ch. 5, n. 11). Nevertheless, they survived in pockets of Europe as late as the seventeenth century, as is shown by an indignant entry in the English *Calendar of State Papers* for the year 1608. One Lord Howard, a known recusant, being elected a Christmas Lord of Misrule, with his tenants and servants in Bampton, Westmoreland,

> most grossly disturbed the minister in time of Divine Service. . . .
> These Christmas misrule men, some of them drank to the minister when he was at prayers; others stepped into the pulpit and invited the parishioners to offer for the maintenance of their sport; others came into the church disguised; others fired guns and brought in flags and banners; others sported themselves with pies and puddings in the church using them as bowls in the church aisles; others played with dogs, using them as they used

to frighten sheep; and all this done in church in time of Divine
Service, and the said Lord doth bring the ministers about him into
contempt, scorn, and derision.

The influence of this carnival tradition is unmistakable in
Marlowe's historical tragedy *Edward II*. In the first scene the young
king and his lover, Gaveston, boldly act out the game of the mock
bishop and lord. Edward gets Gaveston to throw the Bishop of
Coventry into an open sewer and then, in all seriousness but with an
obvious sneer at the humiliated bishop, confers on Gaveston a string of
grand offices and titles, including that of Bishop of Coventry. Echoes
of the same carnival tradition in *Doctor Faustus* are not so precise as
this, but they are more sustained. There is a touch of the riotous cleric
and mock bishop in the characterization of the protagonist almost
from the moment he determines to "be a divine in show" (1.3): it is
apparent in the huge discrepancy between his natural limitations and
the role he aspires to and in the shocking irreverence and mischievous
topsy-turvydom that colors his magical career.

Inversion, as I have intimated, is a fertile source of irony in the
play. Most tragic drama figures a principal character whose imperfect
understanding of the order or power with which he is in conflict is a
source of continuous irony. The classic case is that of Sophocles' *King
Oedipus*, whose impetuous and arrogant hero sins unwittingly against
the gods and from the outset is visibly headed toward a doom to which
he himself is wholly blind. Irony of this kind is very conspicuous in
plays such as *Othello* and *Macbeth* and John Webster's *The Duchess of
Malfi* (c. 1614). But *Doctor Faustus* is arguably the most ironical of all
Renaissance tragedies, and there would seem to be two reasons for
this: first, the inversion principle was inherent in the discourses associated with Marlowe's source narrative, and second, dramatic irony at
its most characteristic entails inversion as reversal, things turning out
to be the exact opposite of what seems or is expected.

The spirit of ironic inversion is apparent in *Doctor Faustus* from
the outset. Almost playful and mock-censorious, it ripples strangely
through the opening chorus, which outlines "the form of Faustus' fortunes good or bad." The seemingly casual phrase "good or bad" is the

first indication of a radical instability in the meaning of key words, and in the relationship between opposites, that will subsequently be disclosed in a profusion of puns and oxymora. The chorus claims that the play will not deal with "proud audacious deeds" and "the dalliance of love," but its "fruitful plot" will quickly show the reverse to be the case. The chorus tells, too, how Faustus so "graced" the "fruitful plot of scholarism" that he surpassed all others in theological dispute and so "was graced"—a technical academic term—"with doctor's name"; the rest of the speech, however, suggests that this "grace" (i.e., academic honor), being grounded in competitive pride, is the very cause of his loss of grace in the only sense of the word that should matter to a theologian. The despairing cry of the penultimate scene is thus anticipated already: "Hell strives with grace for conquest in my soul" (12.55). The key quibble, however, is about the word *heaven*. In "vaunt[ing]" tones that lightly mock the arrogant style of Faustus in advance, the chorus promises that the "heavenly verse" of "our Muse" (pagan deity of poetic inspiration) will show how the "melting heavens" reacted against this Icarus who falls from "heavenly matters of theology" to "a devilish exercise" (chor.1.1–23). Here is anticipated the request and the punning oxymoron that signal the defeat of grace by hell in the penultimate scene:

> That I might have unto my paramour
> That *heavenly Hellen* which I saw of late,
> Whose sweet embracings may extinguish clean
> These thoughts that do dissuade me from my vow:
> And keep mine oath I made to Lucifer.
> (12.75–78; italics and B-text spelling added)

The Prologue intimates in advance, then, that Faustus's up is down, his grace is dis-grace, his heaven is hell, and his first scene fully confirms this. Determining to be from now on "a divine in show," he proceeds to his blasphemous pun: "Divinity adieu!" (1.32). Claiming to have mastered the art of logic, he constructs an illogical argument. Ignoring the second term in the damnation-salvation antitheses of Paul's and John's epistles, he concludes that "divinity is . . . unpleasant harsh, contemptible, and vile" (1.109), while "necromantic books are heavenly" (1.50). Claiming not to deceive himself (1.43), he deceives himself grossly.

Faustus's second scene consolidates the inversion process. In the ritual of conjuration with which it opens (3.1–23), he commits himself to the religion of hell with a bold travesty of the divine. He prays and sacrifices to the devils. Within his magic circle he "racks" or "anagrammatizes" the names of God and saints. He bids farewell to the Trinity and parodies a famous ancient hymn—"Come, Holy Spirit, fill the hearts of thy faithful, and enkindle in them the fire of thy divine love"—in his invocation of the demonic trinity, Belzebub, Demogorgon, and Mephastophilis. When a devil appears in the appropriately hideous form of a dragon, he rebukes him as being "too ugly to attend on me" and commands him to go and return an old Franciscan friar since "that holy shape becomes a devil best" (3.24–27): a nice anti-Catholic jest, but one that works at another level against himself. When the devil obeys him, Faustus in one short sentence throws off two oxymoronic puns that crystallize the gravity and depth of his confusion: "I see there's virtue in my heavenly words!" (3.28). In the great dialogue with Mephastophilis that follows, he matches the demon's desperate gravity with insolent levity, reducing man's "glorious soul" to a "trifle" (3.51, 62), dismissing eternal torment as a bearable discomfort and even claiming that he "confounds hell in Elysium" (3.60, 85–88). One distinguished critic has argued that *Doctor Faustus* dramatizes blasphemy as heroic endeavor, a Promethean enterprise.[3] And there is a general recognition among critics that the carnivalesque usually functions in the drama of this period (as in Shakespeare's *Henry IV*) to challenge orthodox values.[4] What is subverted here is not orthodoxy, however, but one man's reconstructed vision of what is perceived within the world of the play as reality. Faustus's behavior can hardly be termed heroic. It seems less like the behavior of a Prometheus (who stole fire from the gods to the great benefit of all humankind) than of an intoxicated daredevil dancing at the edge of a precipice before his inevitable disappearance. Marlowe gives us a strange and wholly unique vision of terrifying folly and foolery. To characterize such behavior as heroic and Promethean is, I believe, to diminish its singularity.

Faustus's signing of the deed of gift is also represented as a willful inversion of the sacred in which blasphemy and blindness combine. The scene opens with a soliloquy in which Faustus struggles to overcome the voice of conscience, which has begun to trouble him (5.1–14). The inversion principle informs this struggle throughout. Faustus tells himself that to turn to God is to "go . . . backward," an echo of the Evil Angel's first words in the opening scene: "Go forward Faustus in that famous art" (1.74). Thoughts of "heaven, and heavenly things," he insists, and his Evil Angel reasserts, are "vain fancies," "illusions, fruits of lunacy, / That makes men foolish that do trust them most," whereas thoughts "of honour and of wealth" are, by implication, solid realities (5.4, 18–21). He must "despair in God and trust in Belzebub," to whom he will "build an altar and a church, / And offer luke-warm blood of new-born babes." Having thus deified the diabolical, Faustus confirms his allegiance to Lucifer in familiar biblical phrases that originally signified faith in Christ and his saving grace. Asking rhetorically, "When Mephastophilis shall stand by me, / What god can hurt thee Faustus?" he echoes what St. Paul wrote to the Romans in his account of justification by faith: "If God be for us, who is against us?" (Rom. 8.31). Telling Mephastophilis to "come . . . and bring glad tidings from great Lucifer" (5.26–27), he identifies his familiar with the angel who announces the coming of the Savior (Luke 2.10), and Lucifer with the Savior himself.

In the process of inverting spiritual reality, Faustus has now quoted twice from Paul's Epistle to the Romans (see p. 37), probably the most authoritative and influential document in the formation of Christian theology. Among other things, it was the major source for the Christian conception of the relationship between God and man as a binding commitment—a testament, will, or covenant. This conception originates in the Old Testament, where God, having released his chosen people from captivity to the heathen, established a new relationship with them by means of his covenant—the Decalogue, or "the Law." In the Christian dispensation, however, fallen man is seen as condemned by the law and in bondage to sin before the coming of

Christ. Man is released thereafter and given the freedom of the sons of God by virtue of the new covenant or testament—that is, Christ's saving blood, the testament of hope and redemption, the price demanded by the terms of the covenant for such generosity being simply filial obedience (see especially Rom. 5–8 and Mark 14.24). The Epistle to the Romans, where the theme of the new covenant is embedded in an eloquent plea for faith in the justifying grace of Christ, is thus a subtext of major significance in Marlowe's dramatization of Faustus's covenant with Lucifer. For Faustus, who has despaired of the possibility of divine forgiveness and entered deliberately into a state of spiritual bondage, consciously engages here in a ritual travesty and denial of the covenant of Christ's saving blood. Thus, the pact has been anticipated in the opening scene by Faustus's despairing rejection of the Bible (Old and New Testament or Covenant), and of Paul's message in particular, and by his simultaneous expressions of contempt for legacies and the laws of inheritance.

As the representative of a substitute deity, Mephastophilis demands that the signing of the pact be enacted as a grave religious ritual. Faustus must not simply sell the soul that Christ's blood ransomed from bondage (13.92); he "must bequeath it solemnly, / And write a deed of gift" with his "own blood" (5.35–36)—the word *solemnly* being used in its primary sense as meaning "associated or connected with religious rites or observances . . . having a religious character" (*OED*). Faustus stabs his arm and the blood begins to flow, but then "streams . . . not" (5.66). In his final soliloquy he speaks of Christ's saving blood streaming in the firmament, but we do not have to wait for that verbal echo to perceive that this covenantal surrender of his soul to hell is an inversion of Christ's covenantal surrender of himself on the cross. Once the blood begins to flow again, Faustus writes his name and completes the transaction with a sentence in which he quotes Christ's dying words: "Consummatum est, this bill is ended, / And Faustus hath bequeathed his soul to Lucifer" (5.75–76).

Faustus embarks on his career as a necromancer in company with two other black magicians: "So shall the spirits . . . Be always serviceable to us three" (1.122–23). He also conjures up a diabolical trinity when he makes his first approach to the powers of hell. When

Mephastophilis is instructing him in the black art, Faustus says, "Pronounce this thrice devoutly to thy self, / And men in armour shall appear to thee, / Ready to execute what thou desirest" (5.160–62). Given these facts, it may not be without significance that he renews his pact on two more occasions. In many ancient cultures the number 3 was a symbol of fullness, power, and divinity, and of course the Christian deity is a holy trinity. Witchcraft, however, being an oppositional system of belief, appropriated the number 3 from an early age (Hecate/Diana was known as the "triple" goddess; cf. *Midsummer Night's Dream*, 5.2.14), so that this number became a very conspicuous feature of all the rituals of black magic. Shakespeare, it should be noted, was very familiar with this symbolical tradition and may have observed its use in *Doctor Faustus*, for the number 3 is pervasively embedded from the outset in the symbolic design of *Macbeth* (a play whose links with *Doctor Faustus* I have already emphasized): "When shall we three meet again? / In thunder, lightning, or in rain?" (1.1.1–2).[5] It is noticeable, at any rate, that on the third and final confirmation of Faustus's bond with Lucifer the demonic inversion of divine order stands out in harsh relief. It is so managed, too, as to suggest that Faustus is no longer the half-ironic participant in rituals that he is exploiting for his own ends. He has now completely internalized the topsy-turvy worldview that those rituals project.

> (Mephastophilis)
> Thou traitor, Faustus: I arrest thy soul
> For disobedience to my sovereign lord.
> Revolt, or I'll in piecemeal tear thy flesh.
>
> (Faustus)
> Sweet Mephastophilis, entreat thy lord
> To pardon my unjust presumption;
> And with my blood again I will confirm
> My former vow I made to Lucifer.
>
> (Mephastophilis)
> Do it then quickly, with unfeigned heart,
> Lest greater danger do attend thy drift. (12.57–65)

In *The Damnable Life*, a newfound enthusiasm for astrology signals Faustus's turning from God to the devil. Indeed, astrology functions almost as a comprehensive synonym for "the infernal arts": after studying these, Faustus "could not abide to be called Doctor of Divinity, but waxed a worldly man, and named himself an Astrologian" (66–67). Marlowe greatly reinforces this perspective on astrology and assimilates it to the inversion pattern, specifically, to the notion that the way up is the way down. Cornelius tells him that access to the "spirits" and all "the miracles that magic will perform" depends on his being "grounded in astrology" (1.122–23, 137–38). There is a pun on the word *grounded* here—the verb meant not only "to set on a firm basis" but also "to bring to the ground, to knock down" (*OED*)—that converts the phrase into a brilliant proleptic oxymoron. The drift of the pun becomes clear when Faust begins his conjurations and leaps heavenward in imagination, but into an all-enveloping darkness:

> Now that the gloomy shadow of the earth,
> Longing to view Orion's drizzling look,
> Leaps from th' antarctic world unto the sky,
> And dims the welkin with her pitchy breath:
> Faustus, begin thine incantations. (3.1–5)

There is a similar hint at the end of the pact-signing scene when he asks Mephastophilis to "dispute again, and argue of divine astrology" (5.209–10) so that he can escape from tormenting thoughts of salvation and damnation; their learned discussion functions in exactly the same way, he admits, as the enchanting songs of "*blind* Homer," which were sung to help him conquer "deep despair" (3.201–2; emphasis added). Even the lofty style of the second chorus announcing his aerial flights, "to know the secrets of astronomy," has an ironic countermeaning: not only is his brightly burning chariot "yoked" to "dragons' necks" but his attempt to "scale Olympus' top" suggests the mythical pride of the rebellious Titans, destined to be hurled hellward from "Jove's high firmament" (1–5). But the mythical figure of primary importance in this conception of Faustus's tragic fate is that of

Icarus, with whose ambitious flight and disastrous fall the aspirations of the astrologer were specifically identified in Geoffrey Whitney's *A Choice of Emblemes* (1586) (figure 1) and its influential Latin source, Alciato's *Emblematum Liber* (1536).

"Demons," said the *Malleus*, "are readier to appear when summoned by magicians under the influence of certain stars . . . in order to deceive men, thus making them suppose that the stars have divine power or actual divinity; and we know that in days of old this veneration of the stars led to the vilest idolatry" (11). That the names of all the stars mentioned by Mephastophilis and Faustus in their learned dialogue on "divine astrology" are also the names of well-known pagan gods is pointed enough in the context of such discourse, but the point is sharpened by wordplay in Mephastophilis's reference to the planets: "Nor are the names of Saturn, Mars, or Jupiter, / Feigned, but are erring stars" (5.20–21). *Erring* here means "wandering" (from the verb *errare*, "to wander," the Latin term for planets being *stellae errantes*, "wandering stars"). The other sense of the word *erring* is dramatically relevant to the situation of Faustus, entangled as he is in error and identified by Mephastophilis himself with Lucifer, the fallen star. Conceits and similitudes of this kind were well established in theological discourse and would presumably have been easily picked up by Marlowe's audience. The fathers of the church often commented ironically on the pagans' choice of wandering stars as gods; there is a biblical reference to evildoers as "wandering stars" (Jude 13); and a preacher contemporary with Marlowe described heretical theologians as fallen stars, followers of Lucifer who fell not alone but drew other stars with him into darkness.[6]

Also relevant to the inversion pattern is an alternative religious discourse that enthusiastically celebrates the contemplation of the heavenly bodies. In the section on idolatry at the beginning of the Epistle to the Romans, St. Paul declares that the knowledge of God is inscribed in his creation and so is available even to the pagans (the so-called "argument from design"), "for the invisible things of him, that is, his eternal power and Godhead, are seene by the creation of the worlde, being considered in his workes." But, says Paul, the pagans perversely refused to honor the God so revealed and "neither were thankful, but became

Hᴇᴀʀᴇ, Iᴄᴀʀᴠs with mountinge vp alofte,
Came headlonge downe, and fell into the Sea:
His waxed winges, the sonne did make so softe,
They melted straighte, and feathers fell awaie:
 So, whilste he flewe, and of no dowbte did care,
 He mooude his armes, but loe, the same were bare.

Let suche beware, which paste theire reache doe mounte,
Whoe seeke the thinges, to mortall men deny'de,
And searche the Heauens, and all the starres accoumpte,
And tell therebie, what after shall betyde:
 With blusshinge nowe, theire weakenesse rightlie weye,
 Least as they clime, they fall to theire decaye.

Martial. 1.   *Illud quod medium est, atque inter vtrumque, probamus.*
Ouid. Trist. 2.   *Dum petit infirmis nimium sublimia pennis*
                  Icarus, Icariis nomina fecit aquis.
                  Vitaret cælum Phaëton, si viueret, & quos
                  Optauit stultè tangere, nollet equos.

A warning to astrologers. From Geoffrey Whitney's *A Choice of Emblemes* (1586).

vaine in their imaginations, and their foolish heart was full of darkness"; in consequence they fell into idolatry and all its attendant moral corruptions (Rom. 1.20–21). Paul was here following a line of thought made familiar by the Old Testament poets and prophets, most notably in Psalm 19: "The heavens declare the glorie of God, and the firmament sheweth the work of his handes. Daie unto daie uttereth the same, and night unto night teacheth knowledge. There is no speach nor language where their voyce is not heard. Their line is gone forthe through all the earth, and their wordes into the ends of the worlde; in them hathe he set a tabernacle for the sunne." The marginal commentary in the Geneva translation (1560) of the Bible (from which I have quoted) glosses this famous passage as follows: "The heavens are a scholemaster to all nations, be they never so barbarous. The heavens are as a line of great capital letters to show unto us God's glorie."

This biblical tradition was reinforced in the Middle Ages and the Renaissance by a parallel tradition deriving from Plato, who explained that God gave us eyes primarily in order that we might study the "unerring courses" of the heavenly bodies, imitate their perfect order in our thought processes, and so "regulate our own vagaries" (*Timaeus*, 46–47). Casting one's eyes upward to the heavens (in a quite literal sense) in order to arrive at a knowledge of God and nature was one of the great commonplaces of Renaissance cosmography; yet another was the notion that "we must lay before our eyes two bookes which God hath given us to instruct us by, and to lead us to the knowledge of himselfe, namely the book of nature, and the booke of his worde."[7] These two commonplaces were eloquently illustrated in the 1590s by the successful astrologer George Hartgill, who, in the title page of his book of astronomical tables, *Generall Calendars* (1594), offered an emblematic picture of "The Christian Philosopher," standing erect, looking upward, and holding in one hand the Bible and in the other an armillary sphere, a metallic imitation of the Ptolemaic universe, used in teaching astronomy (figure 2). Icons such as this derived additional force in their cultural context from the fact that "looking up" had always been emblematic of prayer in the Christian tradition; indeed, as Rowland Wymer has shown, it became conventionalized on the Elizabethan and Jacobean stage as a symbol of Christian hope.[8]

The Christian Philosopher, saying, "I shall meditate upon the word and works of Jehovah," and holding the Bible ("The Word of God") in one hand, and an armillary sphere in the other. From the title page of George Hartgill, *General Calendars* (1594).

Taking a hint perhaps from *The Damnable Life*, which records that Faustus "looked up to heaven, but saw nothing therein; for his heart was so possessed with the Devil" (93), Marlowe exploits the tradition of the upward-looking Christian philosopher in the dialogue on "divine astrology" (5.167–87, 210–40), and again in the final scene. Although Faustus has perverted his study of the heavens by invoking demonic assistance, that study nevertheless still reminds him perforce of a divinely constructed order and harmony. Holding in his hand the astrological book given him by Mephastophilis, Faustus suddenly declares, "When I behold the heavens, then I repent, / And curse thee wicked Mephastophilis, / Because thou hast deprived me of those joys" (where "the heavens" and "heaven" are implicitly and significantly one). But Faustus's thoughts of repentance and God's pity are subverted by the devil's sophistical response and his own despair. Thus, when he returns to the subject of the heavens, he does so in a merely inquisitive and disputatious spirit calculated to exclude thoughts of the Creator. Yet these thoughts continue to force themselves upon him. In answer to Faustus's questions, Mephastophilis explains that the spheres, "mutually enfolded in each other's orb," all "jointly move upon one axeltree . . . from east to west in four-and-twenty hours upon the poles of the world." This prompts Faustus to remark on the double motion of the planets, "the first finished in a natural day," the second finished in fixed periods (varying from 28 days to 30 years) for each planet: he acknowledges, in other words, that although the planets may wander, they may do so only within specified local and temporal limits ("both *situ et tempore*"). Such reflections inevitably lead Faustus to a demand with which the demon angrily refuses to comply, "Tell me who made the world," and beyond that to a prayer that we must assume is uttered with an earnest upward look: "Ah Christ, seek to save / Distressed Faustus' soul" (5.257–58). The response to this prayer seems to suggest that Faustus's spiritual condition is irremediably upside down, for it is answered by the immediate appearance of the unholy trinity, Lucifer, Belzebub, and Mephastophilis. Overcome by Lucifer's contention (itself a brazen inversion of the truth), "Christ cannot save thy soul, for he is just. / There's none but I have interest in the same" (5.259–60), Faustus begs "pardon" of his demonic master and then

> vows never to *look to heaven*,
> Never to name God, or to pray to him,
> To burn his Scriptures, slay his ministers,
> And make my spirits pull his *churches down*.
> (5.268–72; italics added)

The downward significance of Faustus's astrological flight and upward gaze is brought home with unparalleled intensity in the paralysis and claustrophobia that overtake him in the last scene (13.59ff.). Faustus conjures the heavenly spheres to "stand still" so that "time may cease and midnight never come," but the stars "move *still*"—and wordplay enacts once again the process of inversion. He urges the stars that reigned at his nativity to "draw up Faustus like a foggy mist . . . so that my soul may but ascend to heaven." The command is futile, however, and he remains grounded in astrology. As if recalling the Second Scholar's advice to "look up to heaven, remember God's mercies are infinite" (13.13), Faustus turns to the heavens as a theologian rather than an astrologer, yet the same fate awaits him: "O I'll leap up to my God! Who pulls me down?" It is as if the opening words of his first conjuration are being turned back upon him:

> Now that the gloomy shadow of the earth,
> Longing to view Orion's drizzling look,
> Leaps from th' antarctic world unto the sky,
> And dims the welkin with her pitchy breath:
> Faustus, begin thine incantations,
> And try if devils will obey thy hest. (3.1–6)

Clearly the actor who plays Faustus must look upward in the last soliloquy with agonizing desire, but he must also withdraw his eyes in terror from what he imagines he sees there and then look compulsively earthward:

Woodcut from the title page of the 1616 edition of *Doctor Faustus*.

> see where God
> Stretcheth out his arm, and bends his ireful brows!
> Mountains and hills, come, come and fall on me,
> And hide me from the heavy wrath of God.
> No, no?
> Then will I run headlong into the earth.
> Earth, gape! (13.77–82)

The woodcut given on the title page of the 1616 edition of *Doctor Faustus* (figure 3) shows the protagonist with a magician's rod in his right hand, a book of the black arts in his left, and an armillary sphere behind him. He stands enclosed within a magic circle decorated with occult symbols. He is not looking upward but is watched by the dragon that he has conjured from below and displaces, as it were, the image of the crucifix before it on the wall. Faustus here is the antithesis of "The Christian Philosopher" who gazes heavenward with "The Word of God" in his right hand and the armillary sphere in his left, declaring, "I shall meditate on the word and works of Jehovah" (figure 2). In many productions of the play, Faustus's magic circle is boldly and centrally represented on the stage floor. For a Renaissance audience, fully attuned to the discourses within which this play was written, it would have seemed emblematically appropriate if, at the end, before he is carried off "quick" by the devils, Faustus were standing transfixed within his circle, looking downward to see "ugly hell gape" (13.109, 114).

7

Lusion, Illusion, Delusion

DOCTOR FAUSTUS, THEATRICALITY, AND POSTMODERNIST CRITICISM

By far the most influential play during the English Renaissance was *The Spanish Tragedy*, written (c. 1585–90) by Thomas Kyd, the unfortunate playwright who was imprisoned, tortured, and professionally ruined as a consequence of having shared lodgings with Marlowe (see Chronology). One of the most remarkable features of this tragedy is its overt theatricality: its consciousness of itself as drama; its presentation of dramatic entertainments as part of the plot; its continuous use of metaphors that emphasize the resemblance between life and the stage, action and acting, intrigue and plot. There is no theatricality of this kind in Marlowe's *Tamburlaine the Great*. Due in some measure no doubt to the enormous popularity of Kyd's play, the ludic conception is conspicuous in Marlowe's later work: in *Edward II* and, most notably, in *The Jew of Malta* and *Doctor Faustus*. As most students of Shakespeare and his successors are aware, too, theatricality was to become a characteristic feature of Renaissance drama as a whole.

It was not until the 1960s and after that critics began to pay close attention to the self-consciously theatrical element in Renaissance drama (Shakespeare and the Jacobeans, rather than Marlowe, first attracted attention). They did so to a very large extent because it echoed certain leading preoccupations in the intellectual life of the period. These preoccupations derived from sociological role theory and, later, from poststructuralist and Marxist theories of the self or "subject." (Their prevalence in the United States and France during this period owed much to a general sense of disillusion and skepticism generated by the Algerian and Vietnam wars and to a related awareness of the extent to which the individual is at the mercy of the state and its mystifying ideologies.) Role theory suggested that the self is a bundle of roles and that identity is socially bestowed. It encouraged the systematic analysis of social behavior and social structures on the model of drama, in which all action and all roles are prescribed. Role theory thus undermined the commonsense notion of the continuity of the self; it also presented a radical challenge to the humanist emphasis on the ability of men and women freely to shape—in some measure—their own lives and selves.

Postructuralist and Marxist theories of the subject followed easily in the wake of role theory. Marxism insists that human consciousness is determined by social being and not vice versa. It rejects both the idea of a basically unchanging human nature and the notion of an autonomous, unified, continuous self. Deconstruction's attack on the idea of the unified and stable self followed inevitably from its rejection of structures and of determinate meaning in language: the floating, playful signifier, the endless play of *différance* (where the meaning of every word is dependent on the meaning of another and another and so on), and the notion of perceived reality as mere text, combined to produce the conception of the floating, playful, textualized self.

It is easy enough to detect this complex of ideas at work in the more familiar interpretations of the play element in *Doctor Faustus*, some of which, for reasons to be explained later, I should like to summarize and evaluate at this point. Stephen Greenblatt's we have already touched on; it is not the most extensive, but it is certainly the most influential. Like all Marlowe's heroes, Greenblatt explains,

Faustus struggles to fashion an identity for himself, but in vain; his self is constructed by the dominant culture against which he rebels, but the "theatrical energy" and the "histrionic extremism" that characterize his self-fashioning acts distinguish him from everyone else in the society to which he belongs. This frenetic endeavor to create an identity is expressive, too, of a loss of all belief in transcendent reality, a metaphysical despair that suggests that "all objects of desire are fictions, theatrical illusions shaped by human subjects." Thus, like Marlowe's other heroes, Faustus courageously copes with consciousness of the void that awaits him by means of a destructive delight in role-playing, by entire absorption in the game at hand: "This is play on the brink of the abyss, absolute play" (214–21). Greenblatt's study thus encompasses in its interpretive frame of reference not only the socially constructed, multiple self projected by social anthropology, Marxism, and poststructuralism but also the joyous epistemological nihilism of Jacques Derrida and his forebear Friedrich Nietzsche. One recalls in particular Derrida's approval (in "Structure, Sign and Play in the Discourse of the Human Sciences") of "the Nietzschean *affirmation*, that is, the joyous affirmation of the play of a world of signs without fault, without truth, and without origin."[1]

Simon Shepherd builds on Greenblatt's ideas but has his own, characteristically Marxist stance. He, too, finds in the play element of this tragedy a concern with the social construction of the self; even the comic action, when Faustus appears to have his leg pulled off ("I am undone!"), exposes the myth of the unitary subject and shows how "identity is made and readily unmade."[2] Marlowe's dramatization of show and spectacle, with an onstage audience watched by an offstage one, is a proto-Brechtian device that intensifies a prevailing deconstruction of meaning; this in turn contradicts the attempts of religious figures in the drama to impose a coherent pattern of behavior on Faustus, a character "moved by the *endless* inter*play* of desire and dissatisfaction" (98; emphasis added). Shepherd's emphasis, however, is more political than psychosociological or philosophical. What the play element in the tragedy primarily signifies for him is "delight as repression, pleasure as deception" (101), a political phenomenon of allegedly substantial importance in Elizabethan society. Just as the devils distract Faustus from thoughts of repentance by means of play and

illusion, just as Faustus himself uses magical illusion to silence a critical knight and charm a group of clowns into a state of comical dumb-
ness, so the Elizabethan ruling class used theater to help the people
forget the real conditions of their lives, to silence skepticism, and to
"manipulate . . . exploit and silence" the lower class (103). Marlowe,
Shepherd implies, wryly concedes that what he and his fellow playwrights are really doing is distributing opium to the masses.

Roger Sales builds respectfully on both Greenblatt and Shepherd
in what is undoubtedly the most thoroughgoing account of the theatrical element in the play: role-theory determinism, deconstructive epistemological nihilism, and a Marxist vision of Elizabethan society as a
system of repression are all in evidence.[3] Marlowe's plays are historically contextualized in a society where public life is conceived of as a
"Theatre of Hell": a world of espionage, conspiracy, treason trials,
staged public punishments and executions (the latter being seen
through the lens of that key poststructuralist text, Michel Foucault's
Discipline and Punish, especially its chapter on "The Spectacle of the
Scaffold"). In poststructuralist fashion, Sales sees Marlowe's historical
setting not as context but as text—dramatic text, however. Everything
in this society, he explains, was dramatized. His view of the Elizabethan
political play text allows him to see Faustus and the Elizabethan playwright as mirror images of each other. Like the playwright, Faustus is a
kind of vagrant or masterless man (a type viewed by the Elizabethan
authorities as a dangerous source of social instability). Like the playwright, he is socially marginalized, the grove in which he conjures being
comparable to the public theaters located in the Liberties, or outskirts
of London. Just as the Elizabethan playwright is rescued from his politically vulnerable, masterless condition by royal or aristocratic patronage, so Faustus is given employment and a place in society by Lucifer,
whose concerns and tactics are those of a Renaissance prince (141–44).
Like any such prince, Lucifer legally binds his subject to him in order to
prevent him from rebelling and allows him little in return. As Faustus's
performances show, all theatricality does is to fill empty spaces. Despite
his early fantasies of imperial conquest, Faustus remains "dependent
upon patronage" (153). He is a mere entertainer, playing at best to
coterie audiences and producing shows that do nothing to change the
world (152–53). Finally, he is reduced from playwright to actor, being

"condemned to play the part that has been written for him in the theatre of Hell. He must deliver his dying speech from the scaffold and then meet his executioners" (158).

I have felt it necessary to summarize these kindred approaches to the theatricality of *Doctor Faustus* for three reasons: because they are representative of current critical trends, because they differ greatly from the interpretation I have to offer, and because I believe them to be profoundly misleading. Perhaps the most striking aspect of Greenblatt's commentary is its distance from the text. Although he coins memorable phrases on the hero's theatricality, never once does he quote, or even allude to, any of the numerous passages in the text where theatrical performance or theatrical metaphor is involved. Also, his use of the role metaphor is not determined and controlled by the text; rather, it is brought to the text and freely applied. His remarks on desperate role-playing and energetic theatricality refer to *Tamburlaine* as well as *Doctor Faustus*, even though there are no staged plays and no theatrical metaphors in *Tamburlaine*: as in Sales's book, sociological role theory, with its notorious tendency to kidnap all human behavior indiscriminately, takes precedence over the texts and blurs the distinctive significances of each. Furthermore, although he begins his chapter on Marlowe with a lengthy quotation from a contemporary document exemplifying Elizabethan colonialist endeavors, thus defining his method as rigorously historical, Greenblatt makes no attempt whatever to locate the theatricality of *Doctor Faustus* in the theological discourse or the dramatic tradition to which it belongs. This lack of textual and contextual constraint means in effect that instead of the interpretive frame serving to illuminate the text, the text serves rather to give body to the ideas on which the frame is based. For those familiar with Marlowe, Greenblatt's striking phrases point much less obviously in the direction of *Doctor Faustus* than (as suggested earlier) in that of Nietzsche, Foucault, Derrida, and social theorists such as Clifford Geertz and Irving Goffman.

The interpretations offered by Shepherd and Sales reflect the difficulty of extracting a primarily political interpretation from a primarily religious text. The two critics respond to this problem in much the same way as did those grave men in the Middle Ages and the Renaissance who felt it necessary to find moral edification in the erotic, mythological tales of Ovid: they allegorize the text. But there is no hint in Marlowe's play that it should be construed allegorically; the political allegory is arbitrarily imposed on it. Unlike Greenblatt, however, both Shepherd and Sales do make forays into the text, yet when they do so, the interpretations they draw tend to fit only the immediate context and to produce contradiction when pursued in relation to the rest of the text. As with Faustus himself, selective quotation brings short-term benefits only. For example, since Faustian illusion makes public fools of the emperor and a knight, it does not make sense to see a specifically working-class victimization in its fooling of the clowns. Indeed, the whole argument that play should be seen as an instrument used by a cynical ruling class to keep the rest of the people in a state of political passivity is invalidated by the fact that the emperor is the most enthusiastic and most grateful, as well as one of the most deluded, admirers of Faustus's art. (The enthusiasm of the English aristocracy for dramatic entertainments of all kinds corresponds with the emperor's enthusiasm and further weakens the play-as-political-repression argument.) In Sales's interpretation, too, explicit identification of the devils with the Elizabethan ruling class problematizes the significance of God, the Good Angel, and the Old Man, all of whom oppose Faustus's addiction to play and illusion, and all of whom, in a politically subversive allegory, would be expected to represent the dominant order. How can they be accommodated to the political argument? Where do they fit in? The question is ignored.

DEVILRY AND THEATRICALITY IN CHRISTIAN TRADITION

In what follows, I shall attempt to offer a reading of theatricality in *Doctor Faustus* that is consistent with the play as a whole and that is inductively drawn from both the play's verbal and nonverbal language and its own discursive and dramatic contexts.[4] A helpful starting point for such a reading will be an account of the relationship between the terms given in the title of this chapter. Whereas the word *ludic* is a fairly familiar newcomer to our language, the word *lusion* has long since come and gone. Most Latinists like Marlowe would have known what it meant, but it was included in a dictionary of hard words in the midseventeenth century, where it was defined as "a playing, game, or pastime" (see *OED*). It is worth recording here because it serves to draw attention to a basic affinity between the ideas of play, illusion, and delusion that is fundamental to *Doctor Faustus* and its cultural matrix: all three of the associated words derive from the Latin *ludere* (to play) and *ludus* (play, drama). The verb *illude* (now obsolete) and the noun *illusion* in its first and now obsolete sense have a meaning that is also very relevant here: "mockery, derision, making sport of." (Pertinent to this context, *OED* cites "it illudes, or mockes the worshippers of these Idols," and "illudyd by the goddesse . . . Dyan.") Since *illude* also signifies tricking, imposing upon, deceiving with false hopes, deceiving the bodily or the mental eye by false prospects (*OED*), it also comes very close to the word *delude*, which means to play with someone to his injury or frustration, to befool the mind or judgment, or (a sense now obsolete) to mock, deride, or laugh at.

The ideas of play, game, acting, and mocking laughter were all associated with the devil almost from the beginnings of Christian thought down to the sixteenth century. Even in early Latin treatises on the spiritual life the words *ludere*, *illudere*, and *deludere* are constantly used as synonymous terms for the devil's attempt to ensnare the soul. The relationship between the soul and its enemy is seen both as a gladiatorial contest and a theatrical or illusionary event where the victor triumphantly derides the deluded victim or the unmasked attacker.[5] This identification of evil in serious discourse with game, contest, and theatrical play might seem paradoxical. The explanation for the paradox lies mainly in the fierce hostility of the church fathers to the pagan "spectacles" (plays, games, and gladiatorial contests). Associated as they were with the cults of the old gods, these spectacles were condemned as part of Satan's endeavor to win the faithful back into idolatry. In their attacks on pagan spectacle, the church fathers deployed Plato's well-known arguments against drama and rhetoric for their own purposes and, in the process, gave to the Christian myth of the devil its characteristic features. By a reverse process, the diabolical tempter and accuser of biblical tradition became a creature of boundless, disordered energy, and also a theatrical and oratorical artist who ensnares his victims by means of beguiling shows, cunning impersonations, and persuasive speech. This model of the demonic evil is commonplace in the religious literature and folklore of the Middle Ages. It lies behind the sportive, histrionic, and smooth-tongued Vice of the morality plays and through him exercised a great influence on Renaissance drama. However, since traditional demonology was still very much alive in the sixteenth century, as the witchcraft mania testifies, the conception of evil as sportive and histrionic would probably have affected the dramatists' representation of temptation, corruption, and villainy anyhow.

Other aspects of the devil myth are of relevance to the student of *Doctor Faustus*. Particularly important is the affinity between the demon, the magician, and the actor. All three were condemned in antitheatrical discourse as masters of illusion and transformation bent on glamorizing the immoral and making evil seem good. Significant, too, is the fact that in Puritan diatribes against the stage in the sixteenth and seventeenth centuries, all the old arguments that the church fathers had mobilized against the diabolical art of drama were reproduced and given fresh currency.[6] The playwrights therefore would have been fully acquainted with the ideological basis of the antitheatrical movement. The chief means they employed to counter antitheatrical propaganda was to accept and dramatize the theological identification of play with treacherous change and mere evil, and in so doing to distinguish implicitly between play that deludes for wicked purposes and play that works in the service of truth and morality by unmasking theatrical vice and villainy. All the defenses of the drama failed, of course. With the defeat of the king's party, the Puritans had their way, and the playhouses were closed in 1642 for about 18 years.

PLEASANT SIGHTS AND UGLY HELL

In the Elizabethan conception of drama, much emphasis was placed on the element of show and spectacle: what attracts the eye. This fact is very pertinent to *Doctor Faustus*, a play that dramatizes ocular experience to a unique degree ("looking heavenward" is only part of that experience). We are continually made conscious of the eye, of what it beholds, likes, and dislikes; how it reacts and affects the mind; how it is attracted, fascinated, repelled, manipulated, and misused. Anyone responsive to Marlowe's numerous biblical allusions and alert to this ocular emphasis is likely to be reminded of two well-known passages referring to the dangers associated with the eye, passages well established in the discourse that is most relevant to *Doctor Faustus*. One of the passages (already referred to) is the description of the forbidden fruit as "good for meat, and . . . pleasant to the eyes," and the serpent's assurance that if it is eaten "your eyes shall be opened, and ye shal be as gods" (Gen. 3.5–6). It is impossible not to recall this passage when, for example, Lucifer offers to entertain Faustus with a pageant of the Seven Deadly Sins. A delighted Faustus exclaims, "That sight will be as pleasing unto me, as Paradise was to Adam," and Lucifer sharply tells him to forget about Paradise and "mark this show; talk of the devil and nothing else"; and Faustus, having seen the show, declares, "O this feeds my soul" (5.277–80, 336).

The other passage occurs in the short First Epistle of John (one of the two biblical texts quoted and misinterpreted by Faustus in his opening soliloquy). Addressing young men, John tells them not to "love the worlde, neither the things that are in the worlde. If any man love the worlde, the love of the Father is not in him. For all that is in the worlde (as *the lust of the flesh, the lust of the eyes, and the pride of life*) is not of the Father, but is of the worlde. And the worlde passeth away, and the lustes thereof" (1 John 2.15; emphasis added). Taken up and quoted by a multitude of Christian moralists and preachers, the key phrase here in relation to Faustus—mockingly described by Mephastophilis as a "fond [i.e., foolish] worldling" embroiled in "a world of idle fantasies" (B.103)—is, of course, the parenthetical trinity.

From the beginning of the play to the end, Faustus's enslavement by the devils is intimately associated with his love of what is pleasant to the eye and his corresponding hatred or fear of what is not. His visual problems are primarily found in his response to two things, books and shows. In the first scene he takes up Justinian's book of universal law and dismisses it as offering no more than "external trash"

(1.36). He then takes up "Jerome's Bible" and adjures himself, in a phrase that is to become a refrain in the play, to "view it well" (1.38). But he does not view it well; seeing only what is "hard" in the epistles of John and Paul, Faustus dismisses the Bible in its entirety as "unpleasant, harsh, contemptible, and vile" (1.41, 110). Conversely, he is "ravished" by the enchanting arabesques—"lines, circles, schemes, letters and characters"—of the necromantic book that he presently scrutinizes, and so judges its subject to be "heavenly" (1.50–51, 110).

In his first scene with Mephastophilis, Faustus's weakness and fallibilty are again shown in ocular form. He insists that he must not be attended by an "ugly" familiar; he infers from the fact that Mephastophilis makes an appearance on being conjured that he has power over him; and he sees only what he wants to see, denying the existence of hell to a suffering devil who stands before him in person. But it is in his second encounter with Mephastophilis, when the deed is signed, that his capacity for deception and self-deception is most conspicuously associated with seeing and not seeing; here the book (both the book of truth and the book of fantasies) and the show are collectively foregrounded. Faustus is initially moved toward the fatal deed by the Evil Angel's claim that thoughts of contrition, prayer, and repentance are "illusions, fruits of lunacy, / That make men foolish that do trust them most" (5.18–19). The ironic inversion is obvious enough, and it provides an excellent pointer to the significance of what follows. Preparing to sign his covenant with Lucifer (his anti-Bible), Faustus says, "View here the blood that trickles from mine arm." When it mysteriously stops flowing, he refuses to read the omen correctly and instead blasphemously quotes from the Bible ("*Consummatum est*"). When a second and more explicit omen appears ("*Homo fuge*" ["Fly, O man"]: probably another biblical echo), Faustus responds with a biblical quotation, which in its original context stresses the ubiquity of God ("Whither should I fly?"). He tries to tell himself that his "senses are deceived," and then admits, "I see it plain, here in this place is writ, / "*Homo fuge!*"[7] Although Faustus asserts that he will not fly, Mephastophilis senses Faustus's instability and promptly produces his first theatrical distraction. The reverse of

Jerome's Bible and its remembered phrases, this is superficially delight-ful (dancing devils "giving crowns and rich apparel": external trash) and essentially meaningless: "What means this show?" / "Nothing Faustus, but to delight thy mind withal, / And show thee what magic can perform" (5.57–85). In the signing of the deed, which follows the show, Mephastophilis promises to "perform" and "effect all promises" made to Faustus, and the context is such that the word *perform*, in the sense of "to do" or "to act," becomes and remains thereafter a key pun: "the miracles that magic will perform" (1.136) have no more sub-stance than what "your eyes [i.e., the audience] . . . see performed" on stage (chor.3.16–17). It is no accident that the phrase "form and sub-stance" appears in the first sentence of the deed or that Mephastophilis promises in the deed to appear to Faustus in what "form or shape soever he please" (5.96, 103). Faustus is now trapped in the world of delusive, ever-changing, and insubstantial appearances.

The second part of the deed scene reinforces these ideas. Faustus's desire for a wife is answered with a comic-horrific show, a devil "dressed like a woman, with fireworks" (satiric image of a nag-ging wife?), followed reassuringly by the promise of a "bright" and "beautiful" courtesan: "She whom thine eye shall like, thy heart shall have" (5.152–55). This promise is immediately succeeded by another distraction, the gift of a magical book whose "lines" and "circles" will bring wealth and power if only he will "peruse it thoroughly" (5.155–57; B says "peruse it well," thus recalling the original look at Jerome's Bible more exactly).[8] The same pattern is repeated after Faustus's sudden movement of regret and prayer later in the scene: first a terrifying show to soften him up, then a delightful one to dis-tract him, then the gift of a fantastic book. When he prays to Christ, a menacing Lucifer appears ("O what art thou that lookst so terrible?"), frightens him into a renewed expression of allegiance, produces the show of the Seven Deadly Sins mentioned above ("We are come from hell to show thee some pastime" [5.261, 274]), and promises to let Faustus "see hell, and return," since "in hell is all manner of delight." Faustus clearly does not see that he is being "illuded" by this grim iro-nist, but no offstage audience could miss the mocking effect. Before parting, however, Lucifer gives him the book that is to be his passport into the world of shifting and illusory appearances: "In meantime, take this book, peruse it thoroughly, and thou shalt turn thyself into what shape thou wilt" (5.339–42).

Like the witch of popular lore, Faustus becomes a devil-propelled aeronaut. But his global travels are represented as part of the devil's continuing attempt to secure his allegiance by gratifying the lust of his eye. Upon reaching Rome, Faustus recalls "with delight" that he has seen "buildings fair and gorgeous to the eye" in France, Germany, and other parts of Italy, but now he "longs to see the monuments / And situation of bright-resplendent Rome" (7.2, 10, 45–46). (On the pre-Rome travels, the B text has "There did we view the kingdoms of the world, / And what might please mine eye, I there beheld" [B.72].) At the same time, Faustus is to be allowed to play mocking tricks on the pope and his cardinals by making them the victims of optical illusion. (He does not see that their situation mirrors his own.) In the B text, Faustus and his familiar conceive of this trickery in theatrical terms: "Then in this show let me an actor be, / That this proud pope may Faustus' cunning see . . . any villainy thou canst devise . . . I'll perform it Faustus" (B.72–73). Moreover, they subject two of the cardinals to a hoax whereby they are severely punished by the pope—promised "hellish misery"—in consequence of being struck by Mephastophilis "with sloth, and drowsy idleness" as they "turn their superstitious books" (B.74, 78). The pope's angry question "Wherefore would you have me view that book?" (B.77) varies the refrain that goes back to the beginning of Faustus's fall from grace ("Jerome's Bible, Faustus, view it well"), and the import of his words is visually reinforced by the stage direction "Enter the Cardinals with a book." Since critics have never commented on this highly significant complex of images and ideas, one can hardly accuse the B-text author(s) of laboring the point.

Faustus's largely amiable exploits in German courts are prepared for in a formal speech (chorus 3) whose rhetorical structure (using the figure of symploche, where the end repeats the beginning) carefully suggests that everything he does involves the visual and the theatrical. The speech begins, "When Faustus had with pleasure ta'en the view / Of rarest things," and ends, "What there he did in trial of his art / I leave untold: your eyes shall see performed" (lines 1–2, 17–18; cf. B: "Thou shalt see / This Conjurer performe such rare exploits" [Greg, 1213–14]). Faustus's first visit is to the German emperor, in whom we at last meet someone of importance who shares Faustus's lust of the eye. (Robin the clown's desire to "make all the maidens in our parish dance at my pleasure stark naked before me . . . so I shall see more than ere I felt" [6.3–5], we can consider in chapter 8.) The emperor asks Faustus, "Let me see some proof of thy skill, that mine eyes may be witnesses to confirme what mine eares have reported." Thereafter the emperor's relation to Faustus bears an ironic resemblance to that between Faustus and Mephastophilis, both as we saw it at the start and as we shall see it later in the Helen scene. Appealing specifically to Faustus's necromantic powers, the emperor asks to see his ancestor "Alexander the Great, chief spectacle of the world's pre-eminence," together with "his beauteous paramour" (9.6–8, 24–33). Faustus replies that he will do all that "by art and power of my spirit I am able to perform." Conscientiously, however, he explains that he cannot "present before your eyes the true substantial bodies" of the deceased, but only "such spirits as can lively resemble them" (9.39–48). Yet, such is the verisimilitude of the spectacle that the awed emperor takes illusion for reality: "Sure, these are no spirits, but the true substantial bodies of those two deceased princes" (9.66–67).

Again, the B text amplifies and reinforces this central theme, with much emphasis on spectacle. The simple show required by the A text's stage direction "Enter Mephastophilis, with Alexander and his Paramour" is developed into an elaborate pageant of love and conquest introduced by music and a fanfare of trumpets. Alexander is *seen* conquering his enemy and *seen* embracing and crowning his paramour in a show that could be said, in its context, to epitomize the lust of the eyes, the lust of the flesh, and the pride of life. So deluded, too, is the emperor by the show's versimilitude—"so ravished / With sight of this renowned emperor"—that he moves to embrace the two spirits and has to be restrained by Faustus, who exclaims, "My gracious lord, you do forget yourself: / These are but shadows, not substantial" (B.85), words that could be spoken in such a way as to suggest a certain melancholy self-awareness, but that could equally be delivered in a manner that stresses, with piercing dramatic irony, the extent of Faustus's blindness and folly. There is certainly a sharp, ironic pointer to Faustus's folly in trading his soul for illusions when the emperor delightedly catches sight of the mole or wart that "this fair lady, whilst she lived on earth, / Had on her neck." Exclaims the emperor, "Faustus, I see it plain! / And in this sight thou better pleasest me, / Than if I gained another monarchy" (B.85).

The emperor is given an illusionary bonus in Faustus's feat of imitating Diana, patroness of witches, by putting horns on the knight who expresses skepticism about his magical powers. The A text does not cue this incident into the visual-theatrical frame of reference, but the B text does. Says Faustus to Benvolio/Actaeon, "And I'll play Diana and send you horns presently," and the emperor exclaims, "O wondrous sight!" (B.85). The B text provides similar cuing, with additional emphasis on the extravagant valuation of illusory delights, in the scene where Faustus displays his powers for the benefit of the Duke and Duchess of Vanholt: "Thanks, master doctor, for these pleasant sights; nor know I how sufficiently to recompense your great deserts in erecting that enchanted castle in the air; the sight whereof so delighted me, as nothing in the world could please me more" (B.95).

The ocular-theatrical theme climaxes in the two appearances of a devil in the form of Helen of Troy, "the pride of Nature's works" (12.22). Faustus conjures up the first vision in response to his friends' request "to see that peerless dame of Greece" (12.5). In the A text, the First Scholar praises Faustus for "this glorious deed," and in the B text, for "this blessed sight"; in both texts he expresses the hope that Faustus will be "happy and blest . . . evermore" for accomplishing it (the dramatic irony is equally effective either way). Moreover, in the speech of the Old Man in B that follows the departure of the scholars, Faustus is given a warning about mistaking demonic illusion for heavenly reality that pointedly harks back to his crucial inference that whereas divinity is "harsh, contemptible and vile," magic is ravishing, heavenly. Warning Faustus that magic is likely to "charm thy soul to hell" and banish him "from the sight of heaven," the Old Man adds, "It may be this my exhortation / Seems harsh and all unpleasant; let it not, / For, gentle son, I speak it not in wrath . . . but in tender love, /

And pity" (B.101). The Old Man might be Jerome himself, interpreting the epistles of Paul and John correctly.

The second appearance of "heavenly Hellen" is specifically designed to "glut" Faustus's sexual longings and to help him forget spiritual realities (12.73–78). It is prefaced by Mephastophilis's lines neatly twinning the ocular and theatrical motifs: "Faustus, this, or what else thou shalt desire, / Shall be performed in twinkling of an eye" (12.80–81). The scholars had innocently recalled that Helen's "heavenly beauty" cost the Trojans defeat in a ten-year war with the "angry Greeks." Now, in Faustus's ecstatic address (12.81–100), the destructive and hellish implications of the vision are intimated through ironically inappropriate figures of speech: lyric conceit ("Her lips suck forth my soul"), mythological allusion ("Brighter art thou than flaming Jupiter / When he appeared to hapless Semele"), and hyperbole ("Was this the face that . . . burnt the topless towers of Ilium?"). The illusory image is transformed, too, in Faustus's imagination, into the heroine of a new drama. Like the emperor, Faustus is so enchanted for the moment by his vision of a pagan past that he would enter it himself, would "an actor be" in "blind Homer'[s]" (5.202) fictions. Indeed, he would make them present and future realities where acting is action:

> I will be Paris and for love of thee,
> Instead of Troy shall Wittenberg be sacked,
> And I will combat with weak Menelaus,
> And wear thy colours on my plumed crest:
> Yea, I will wound Achilles in the heel,
> And then return to Helen for a kiss . . .
> And none but thou shalt be my paramour. (12.88–93, 100)

Among the various ironies embedded in Faustus's great final soliloquy (13.59–115), where he seeks unavailingly to escape from inexorable reality, are echoes of his fondness for pleasant sights and his dislike of what seems ugly and unpleasant. The daylight, which he calls for as an escape from what darkness brings, is conceived by him as the opening of "fair Nature's eye." He can "see, see where

"Ugly Hell gape not!" Fifteenth-century version of Hell Mouth, an image familiar not only in medieval iconography but also on the stage from the Middle Ages to the Renaissance. Reproduced from *The Book of Hours of Catherine of Cleves* by permission of the Pierpont Morgan Library, New York. M.945, f.97.

Christ's blood streams in the firmament," but, like daylight, it eludes him. Instead, he can "see where God . . . bends his ircful brows." Faustus bids the earth to "gape" and hide him from God's wrath, but God's grim look still follows him—"My God, my God, look not so fierce on me!"—and "ugly hell gape[s]" to receive him in its maw (figure 4). His last complete sentence is "I'll burn my books!": he does not mean (as many have suggested) all his books, all learning, which would not make sense, but rather the necromantic books whose "lines, circles, schemes, letters, and characters" bewitched his eye and mind.

The B text impressively reinforces the lusion-illusion-delusion complex in the last scene by means of staging, props, and action, as well as language. The scene opens with the demonic trinity entering to "view" and "mark" how Faustus "doth demean himself" in his last desperate moments: he is the miserable protagonist of their play. They are probably located above in the gallery, and their attitude toward their "fond worlding" is one of mocking contempt: "How should he be, but in desperate lunacy . . . his labouring brain / Begets a world of idle fantasies, / To overreach the devil. But all in vain" (B.102–3). The trinity watches silently as Faustus acts out with his servant a better version of their relationship with him. Faustus asks Wagner if he has "perused" his will, and a grateful Wagner (who presumably holds the document) replies, "I do yield / My life and lasting service for your love." They are silent, too, as Faustus explains to the scholars that he has willed his soul to Lucifer and Mephastophilis. When the scholars depart urging prayer, Mephastophilis enters to ban such thoughts: "Despair, think only upon hell; / For that must be thy mansion, there to dwell" (B.105). There could be acute demonic mockery in this sentence, linking up Mephastophilis's accusation of "desperate lunacy," with Faustus's love of "divine astrology," and with his playing the part of Diana (Luna, the Moon), goddess of witchcraft. For as Elizabethans with minimal knowledge of astrology could have recalled, *mansion* means not only a "dwelling place" but also "one of the twenty-eight divisions of the ecliptic occupied by the moon on successive days" (see *OED*, which cites Hawes, 1509, "Dyane . . . entered the Crab, her propre mancyon"). Elizabethans would also have recalled their belief that "lunacy" is a form of temporary madness caused by changes of the moon.

There is certainly ironic mockery in what follows, conjoined with a triumphant claim to ocular trickery. The puns here on *passage* (cf. the Evil Angel's "Go forward, Faustus, in that famous art"), on *dam'd*, and on *I*, and the use of the key verb *view*, are all most pertinent:

(Faustus)
O thou bewitching fiend, 'twas thy temptation
Hath robbed me of eternal happiness.
(Mephastophilis)
I do confess it Faustus, and rejoice!
'Twas I, that when thou wer't i' the way to heaven
Dam'd up thy passage; when thou took'st the book
To view the Scripture, then I turned the leaves
And led thine eye.
What weep'st thou? 'Tis too late, despair, farewell.
Fools that will laugh on earth, must weep in hell. (B.105)

After this, the Good Angel and the Bad Angel enter to show, as well as
to describe, the consequences of Faustus's having "loved the world"
instead of "sweet divinity" (B.104–7). A throne, symbolizing the
"resplendent glory" in heaven that could have been his, descends to
the accompaniment of music. Then, "Hell is discovered," according to
a stage direction. Presumably, a trapdoor is opened, with smoke issu-
ing forth, in sharp visual contrast to the ascending throne. The Bad
Angel gleefully enumerates the horrors to be seen below. Noticeable
here is the use (as in chorus 3) of the figure symploche to frame the
idea of hell pains as punishment for the eye's lust. Noticeable, too, is
Faustus's agonized appreciation of that idea:

(Bad Angel)
Now Faustus, let thine eyes with horror stare
Into that vast perpetual torture-house.
There are the Furies tossing damned souls,
On burning forks; there, bodies boil in lead.
There are live quarters broiling on the coals,
That ne'er can die! This ever-burning chair
Is for o'er tortured souls to rest them in.
These, that are fed with sops of flaming fire,
Were gluttons, and loved only delicates,
And laughed to see the poor starve at their gates.
But yet these are nothing. Thou shalt see
Ten thousand tortures that more horrid be.

(Faustus)
O, I have seen enough to torture me. (B.106)

DIVINITY AND MANLY FORTITUDE

The fantasies to which Faustus falls victim can be reduced to two delusions, the more important of which is the belief that magic will make him godlike. For him, the essence of divinity is power. He dismisses the lawful sciences and professions as being fit only for "servile" and "base" creatures (1.36, 109) and chooses magic because it will make him like Jove, "lord and commander" not only of the natural elements but also of demons and men (1.77). Faustus expects to have "servile spirits" who will enable him to eclipse all rivals in the political world, just as he has done unaided in the intellectual. Thus, he will "reign sole king" of the German provinces (1.94) and the emperor will become his deputy or viceroy (4.111).

Faustus's initial attitude toward Mephastophilis is imperious; he requires Mephastophilis to be "always obedient to my will" and "do whatever Faustus shall command" (3.31, 99). Although at first Mephastophilis explains (to no effect) that he can "perform" no more than Lucifer "commands" (3.43), at their next meeting (before signing the deed) he tells Faustus what he wants to hear: "I will be thy slave and wait on thee" (5.46). After the signing, their relationship changes completely: Mephastophilis refuses to grant the request for a wife and to tell him who made the world. Faustus's consequent threat to repent is instantly answered by the terrifying appearance of Lucifer himself, commanding Faustus (in the B text) to act like "an obedient servant" (Greg, 667), which he promptly does. Faustus's expectation of command over earthly leaders is similarly unfulfilled. Such honor as he wins is that due only to a great "performer." Indeed, his relations with the great are essentially servile; any show or trick they ask for he provides with humble eagerness. This extreme contrast between promise and performance, to which there is nothing comparable in *The Damnable Life*, is underlined clearly enough in the A text (9.12–16), but the B text appreciatively strengthens the emphasis. The magician meekly declares there that "poor Faustus to his utmost power" will "love and serve the German emperor" and will "lay his life" at the "holy feet" of Bruno, the emperor's candidate for the papacy; indeed, he is seen to "kneel and kiss the emperor's hand" when taking his leave of him (B.84, 87). His claim that "the emperor shall not live but by my leave" and his contempt for base servility reverberate in the memory with extraordinary force at this point.

Faustus's divine command, then, like Mephastophilis's humble obedience, is mere show and pastime, something that comes and goes in the twinkling of an eye. The other great delusion of which Faustus is the ironic victim is the belief that his rebellious adherence to Lucifer is heroic. He sets himself up at the start as a model of "manly fortitude" in dismissing thoughts of hell (3.86); Mephastophilis later encourages him in this self-conception: "Then stab thine arm courageously . . . be thou as great as Lucifer" (5.49–52). As always in Marlowe's plays, however, the key term for heroic quality is not manliness or courage but resolution, signifying strength of will, the ability to keep one's word and unswervingly follow one's chosen course of action. Thus, Cornelius warns Faustus at the start that "the miracles that magic will perform" will materialize only if "learned Faustus will be resolute" (1.133).

The touch of bombast, however, in Faustus's response to this warning ("As resolute am I in this / As thou to live, therefore object it not") and the way he has to prompt himself when the moment of conjuration arrives ("Then fear not Faustus, but be resolute, / And try the uttermost magic can perform" [3.14–15]) suggest that this resolution has no firm basis in his character, but is really a role assumed to meet the demands of a "desperate enterprise" (1.81). This suggestion is confirmed by the B text, where "desperate resolution" is precisely what brings about the humiliating downfall of the skeptical knight Benvolio, one of Faustus's ironic counterparts:

> If you will aid me in this enterprise,
> Then draw your weapons, and be resolute:
> If not, depart: here will Benvolio die—
> But Faustus' death shall quit my infamy. (B.87)

The parallel is nicely secured by Benvolio's use of the assertive *will* and *shall*. Characteristic of the resolute style ("For *will* and *shall* best fitteth Tamburlaine," declared Marlowe's personification of the resolute type), these words are heard again at their most impressive in the speech where Faustus projects himself into the role of Homeric hero: "Here will I dwell . . . I will be Paris . . . Instead of Troy shall Wittenberg be sacked . . . I will wound Achilles . . . none but thou shalt be my paramour."

Integral to Faustus's conception of himself as a resolute individualist is the belief that he will uncover truths hidden from the rest of humankind. He assumes that at his command, servile spirits will "resolve" all enigmas and mysteries for him. Marlowe's use of the word *resolve* in this sense simultaneously implies the sense of heroic determination. Faustus imagines, and then performs, the part of an imperious interrogator determined to get at the truth of things:

> How I am glutted with conceit of this!
> Shall I make spirits fetch me what I please,
> Resolve me of all ambiguities,
> Perform what desperate enterprise I will? (1.78–81)

> . . . meet me in my study at midnight,
> And then resolve me of thy master's mind. (3.100–101)

> Well, resolve me in this question. (5.237)

But Mephastophilis and Lucifer resolve nothing of importance, and offer Faustus little more than "freshmen's suppositions" and diverting shows that mean "nothing" (5.85, 231).

Instead of resolution, what we quickly begin to perceive in Faustus is a radical instability. When he says to Mephastophilis, "I will renounce this magic, and repent" (5.187), the determined "will" indicates just where the his resolution should be exercised. But Faustus, unable to resist the demonic voices of despair, fails the test. In doing so, however, he protects his heroic self-image by inverting the sense of "resolution," suggesting that to retreat is to advance: "Now go not backward: no Faustus, be resolute, / Why waverest thou?" (5.6–7), and

"Why should I die then, or basely despair? / I am resolved! Faustus shall ne'er repent" (5.207–8). The emptiness of this heroic self-image is painfully exposed in the penultimate scene when his terrified surrender to Mephastophilis's physical threats (provoked by his thoughts of repentance) is sharply contrasted with the defiance of the Old Man to the same threats. The contrast is given additional force by the Old Man's entry in the middle of the Helen speech precisely when Faustus is declaring that he "will . . . combat with weak Menelaus" and "wound Achilles in the heel" (12.88–92). Singularly unheroic, too, is Faustus's spiteful request that the Old Man be tormented for urging him to repent and so exposing him to Mephastophilis's wrath. Most pointed of all, however, is the manner of Faustus's death, carried screaming to hell by the demon whom he lectured on the need for manly fortitude in enduring hell's torments.

Faustus's confused understanding of himself and his desperate enterprise is finely underscored by Marlowe's ironic recognition that in one of its senses the word *resolution* is synonymous with its antonym. It signifies not only fixity and persistence but also disintegration, the breaking up of something into its component parts. Marlowe begins to hint at this contradiction in the scene where Faustus formally binds himself to hell. Urging himself to "be resolute," Faustus declares that the love of Belzebub is "fixed" in him, and then signs the pact (5.6,12); at the same time, Mephastophilis fetches fire to "dissolve" the ominously congealed blood, and is soon admitting that "when all the world dissolves . . . every creature shall be purified" and "all places shall be hell that is not heaven" (5.124–27). Combined with the image of congealed and melted blood (echoing perhaps his "waxen" and "melting" Icarian wings [chor.1.21–22]), the diction here suggests that the resolute Faustus is now one with the spirit of change and dissolution. This idea is presently embodied in one of the play's most important verbal and nonverbal symbols: henceforth, all Faustus's resolves to repent will be instantly undone by the devils' threats to tear him to pieces. (In the B text, this symbol—as anticipated in the comic scenes—acquires a grimly literal status at the end when Faustus's body is discovered "all torn asunder" by the devils whom he served [B.108].) The final irony, however, is not that Faustus's des-

perate resolution has trapped him in the terrors of violent physical dissolution; it is that he dies longing for the dissolution of his soul, bitter-
ly acknowledging that only the souls of dying beasts are "soon
dissolved in elements" (13.106).

ILLUSION AND REALITY

Faustus's engagement with play, then, should not be interpreted as the
efforts of a gifted individual to realize his true potential and construct
an identity in defiance of a society that arbitrarily resists self-fulfillment
and determines identity. Like all authoritarian and stratified societies,
Elizabethan society did function to a considerable extent in that manner. It does not follow, however, that *Doctor Faustus* necessarily
reflects such a process. According to the texts as we have them, it is not
society with its repressive engines and ideologies that resists Faustus but
reality. Faustus's role-playing is simply an attempt to deny or escape
from what he is, both as a human being and as an individual. He seeks
to deny what he is as a human being because omnipotence and omni-
science are not human attributes, and he seeks to deny his individual
identity because in Christian belief that is a function of the soul.

The critic determined to impose a materialist reading on the text
seizes on the comic scene in which Faustus's apparent loss of his leg
prompts the cry "Alas, I am undone" and construes this as subverting
the idea of an essential self. We have seen, however, that an opposite
meaning is to be inferred from the motif of the torn body: as the Old
Man, Mephastophilis, and finally Faustus himself all declare, the body
may be torn, but the self remains with the soul. We may not like this
version of the Faust myth and may feel that the myth could be made to
mirror our deepest concerns more comprehensively. In that case, however, we should leave *Doctor Faustus* as it is and do what countless
imaginative writers have done: write our own version. The most
appropriate comment on the theatricality of the protagonist in
Marlowe's play is provided by the protagonist himself: "My gracious
lord, you do forget yourself: these are but shadows, not substantial
things."

8

Sport

In 1675, Edward Phillips, nephew and pupil of John Milton, attributed the great popular success of *Doctor Faustus* to its "tragical sport" (*MCH*, 51), a phrase in which he seems to be recalling Ben Jonson's punning reference, in his famous eulogy on Shakespeare, to the author of *The Spanish Tragedy* as "sporting Kyd." Great comic dramatist though he was, Jonson, unlike Kyd, Marlowe, and Shakespeare, rigorously excluded "sport" from his own tragedies. However much he admired Shakespeare, he would have wholeheartedly endorsed Milton's position as stated in the preface to his austerely classical tragedy *Samson Agonistes* (1671). Milton explained there that he wished "to vindicate tragedy from the small esteem, or rather infamy, which in the account of many it undergoes at this day . . . happening through the poet's error of intermixing comic stuff with tragic sadness and gravity; or introducing trivial and vulgar persons: which by all judicious hath been counted absurd, and brought in without discretion, corruptly to gratify the people."

Of all the great tragedies of the Renaissance, none offends so palpably as *Doctor Faustus* does against the classical principle of dramatic decorum that Jonson and Milton cherished. Neither does any offend so unashamedly. There are frequent and explicit references in both the A and B texts to "sport," "mirth," "merriment," "frolic," and "rustic gambols." Although the judicious have long since found artistic justification (as well as historical reasons) for intermixing comedy with tragedy in the plays of this period, many—perhaps a majority—would still hold that it is the comic element that makes *Doctor Faustus* a seriously flawed masterpiece. Judged by the standards set by Shakespearean and even Kydian tragedy, the comic element is, they would argue, both unsubtle and excessive: the play begins and ends magnificently, but the middle, where most of the comedy occurs, is on a wholly inferior level of quality. Recently, some critics have argued that this view is essentially a literary one and that what is flat in reading is lively in performance. Indeed, one critic has forcefully contended that the sportive element is often "splendid farce," "beautifully written," and "an essential element in the overall power" of the tragedy.[1] To this, however, some might reply that farce is still a low form of comedy and that there is simply too much of it in this tragedy.

In combination with the related scenes of magical showmanship in the middle section of the play, the comic element has always focused critical attention on the question of authorship. It has been suggested that Marlowe planned the play, wrote the beginning and the end, and then left it to be completed by a collaborator. It has also been suggested that the play was unfinished when Marlowe died and that someone else undertook to complete it, much as Birde and Rowley were assigned to amplify the shorter version some years later. Such hypotheses may be correct, but it seems unwise to advance them on the assumption that Marlowe could not be held responsible for coarse comedy of the practical-joke kind that dominates the play as we have it. He himself had a reputation for outrageous and insensitive jocularity in his relationships with others. Moreover, the first printer of *Tamburlaine the Great* informed the reader that he had "purposely omitted some fond and frivolous gestures, digressing and . . . far unmeet for the matter . . . deformities [which were] a great disgrace to so honourable and stately a history." We have no reason to suppose that Marlowe was not responsible for that frivolous material.

What now seems beyond dispute, however, is that the comic element in *Doctor Faustus*, however disproportionate or unsubtle we might individually judge it in reading or performance, is studiously integrated into the play's pattern of meaning. Thus, to understand the comic scenes is to come to a clearer sense of what the play is about. Moving around the "hermeneutic circle," we interpret the component parts of the text in the light of a prior interpretation of the whole and at the same time refine and justify our prior interpretation of the whole by close inspection of the parts. The appropriate point of departure for the interpreter here is once again, I would suggest, the Christian myth of the devil and the association of the tempter with ideas of play and game. In the previous chapter, we considered the theatrical dimension of the myth, but here our concern is with the larger conception of moral decline as an addiction to immoderate amusement—fun, frivolity, irreverent jocularity, festive indulgence, and revelry. In this perspective, pastime is set in sharp antithesis to time, and time to eternity; diversion is time-wasting, and sensuality a fatal diversion from the urgent spiritual task of saving one's eternal soul. Thus, in the fifteenth-century morality play *Mankind*, the protagonist's mentor, Mercy, opens the play with a solemn adjuration to "divert not yourself in time of temptation, / That you may be acceptable to God at your going hence." His earnest address is interrupted by four noisy vice figures, servants of the devil Titivillus, who play parodistic games with his learned style of speech and urge him to abandon his prayers and join them in song, dance, and "game / . . . in the devil's name": "Let us be merry while we be here!"[2] Mercy himself proves invulnerable to their jesting hedonism, but Mankind does not, and throughout the play his fall from virtue into vice is figured very much as a fall from gravity into the kind of levity that obliterates all thought of his ultimate "going hence."

The most obvious source of comedy in *Doctor Faustus* is the episodes involving clownish characters—whether stupid or shrewd—from the bottom of the social hierarchy, episodes that add up to an instance of what has been called the "clown subplot" in Elizabethan dramatic structure.[3] The comic servants and peasants in these scenes are descended from the vice figures in the moralities (Bevington,

180–81, 253–54). None of them, however, seeks to corrupt Faustus; the Mephastophilis who supports and encourages his diversions in Rome and thereafter resembles the vice much more obviously. But Mephastophilis, of course, is a demon, and as such is a reminder of where the vice's sportiveness originates. He is also a thoroughly untraditional demon at the start, and in his first encounters with Faustus, *Mankind's* distribution of seriousness and levity is inverted: the demon is grave, the protagonist flippant. Faustus is his own jesting vice to begin with, and therein lies a major justification for the different forms of comedy in the play; even when it does not emanate directly from him, the sportive element is always a reflection of the protagonist's spiritual condition. The touch of witty irreverence ("Divinity, adieu!") and of glib sophistry in Faustus's opening soliloquy lay the ground for his extraordinary exhibition of impudent levity in the first scene with Mephostophilis. Here he jokes—to the audience, perhaps—about the efficacy of his blasphemous conjuration ("I see there's virtue in my heavenly words! / Who would not be proficient in this art?"), dismisses men's souls as "vain trifles," and mocks the demon's anguished response to his "frivolous demands" (3.28–29, 62, 83–87). In his next scene with the demon (the pact scene), however, it is noticeable that Faustus privately gives way to feelings of terrified belief in the reality of hell and damnation (5.1–10) before resuming his lighthearted manner:

> (Faustus)
> Thinkest thou that Faustus is so fond to imagine
> That after this life there is any pain?
> Tush, these are trifles and mere old wives' tales.
>
> (Mephastophilis)
> But Faustus, I am an instance to prove the contrary;
> For I am damned, and am now in hell.
>
> (Faustus)
> How, now in hell? Nay, and this be hell, I'll willingly be
> damned here! What, walking, talking, disputing, etc. . . .
> But leaving off this, let me have a wife, the fairest
> maid in Germany, for I am wanton and lascivious. (5.133–41)

What becomes very clear in this exchange (given his prior acceptance of damnation) is that Faustus's jocularity is not at all the product of lighthearted indifference or total skepticism, but the reverse; like his hedonism, with which it will be closely linked from now on, his jocularity functions as a psychological mechanism that helps him to control his fears about the consequences of his proud, audacious deeds. Laughter, like sweet pleasure, helps to conquer deep despair (5.201). We are not dealing at this point with mere farce, crude or refined. We are dealing with humor laced with terror, as the best demonic comedy of medieval narrative and drama had always been.[4]

Mephastophilis's response to Faustus's request for a wife is (as previously noted) a comic-horrific jest. Presenting his "devil dressed like a woman, with fireworks," he asks, "Tell, Faustus, how dost thou like thy wife?" (5.146). This jest marks a change in the demon's consistent gravity of demeanor and prepares for his subsequent relationship with Faustus as partner in a comic duo. In the same scene, Lucifer's "pastime" (5.274) of the Seven Deadly Sins introduces the comedy of the grotesque, corruption visualized as a ludicrous distortion of the natural. Here the mocking and amused manner in which Faustus interrogates the Sins emphasizes his blindness to the fact that they mirror his own condition. This is an effect that obtains much more precisely in all subsequent scenes where he makes others the butt of his humor. There is always an audience that is made to perceive that he is the bigger fool—and an audience beyond that: "Where's thy master?" asks the Scholar, and Wagner replies with chilling wit, "God in heaven knows" (2.4–5).

Faustus uses his magic for the purpose of practical jokery on three occasions, beginning with his invasion of the papal residence in Rome. It is important to note that in his role as comic entertainer he has the audience on his side, for not only is he amusing us but he is doing so at the expense of those who deserve the ridicule to which they are exposed. The audience knows that Faustus is dodging reality, that the follies he debunks in others are also his own, and that he is engaged in activities that betray his grand ambitions. That awareness, however, is only part of a complex response to the immediate action. This process of sympathetic identification is intensified by the perception of a change in his character. In the German scenes, the old arrogance gives way not only to unheroic self-abasement in the presence of "the great" but also to gracious conviviality, a desire to be liked, and a readiness to entertain his friends with spectacles, whether beautiful or sportive. Thus, it becomes much easier for Marlowe to secure complete sympathy for Faustus when he finally confronts the fate that he once so arrogantly derided.

Exposing and deriding arrogance is the whole purpose of his Roman escapade, and the chief element, too, in the dramatic irony that gives artistic justification to this climactic scene. The pope is a caricature of all the pompous pride and worldliness associated with the papacy by Elizabethan Protestants, and Mephastophilis and Faustus set about humiliating him and his "troup of bald-pate friars" with a glee that Marlowe's audience could not but have found engaging. The complexity of audience response, too, would probably have been enhanced by virtue of the fact that this noisy explosion of "sport" and "merriment" (7.49) has all the characteristics of a Feast of Fools or a Boy Bishop revels—a licensed, sacrilegious riot, festive misrule in an ecclesiastical context (see p. 46). The occasion (and this is an addition to the source) is a major church feast; the supreme representative of divine authority is stripped of his dignity and subjected to physical abuse, and sacred ritual—the rite of excommunication—is grossly parodied:

> How! bell, book, and candle; candle book and bell,
> Forward and backward, to curse Faustus to hell.
> Anon you shall hear a hog grunt, a calf bleat, and an ass bray,
> Because it is St. Peter's holy day. (81–84)

But lest the audience lose its necessary measure of detachment at this point, there is the reminder in these lines of Faustus's black-magical inversions ("Jehovah's name / Forward and backward anagrammatized"), and a reminder of his profound spiritual confusion about what constitutes forward and backward. Moreover, the last scene will comment with retrospective irony on Faustus's antics here (depriving the pope of his food and wine, cursing himself) when the blood of redemption eludes his grasp and he is driven in terrible earnestness to curse himself and Lucifer for having "deprived thee of the joys of heaven" (13.106).

The B text's expansion of this scene exploits its theatricality and perceptively increases the ironic analogies between immediate comedy and circumscribing tragedy. Climbing like "proud Lucifer" into his throne on the back of the rival pope elected by the German emperor, the pope declares, "We will depose the Emperor for that deed . . . he grows too proud in his authority, / Lifting his lofty head above the clouds . . . But we'll pull down his haughty insolence" (B.74). The pope condemns his predecessor for having "abuse[d] the church's rites" in giving the emperor power to elect a pope, and lays claim himself to "all power on earth" and even (ridiculously) to all wisdom. "And therefore tho' we would we cannot err" (B.75). Thus, Faustus is involved here with no less than three versions of himself—or four, if we include the echo of Lucifer, whose "aspiring pride and insolence" caused God to throw him "from the face of heaven" (3.68–69). Bruno's prostrate and chained condition, moreover, images the state of humiliating servitude into which Faustus has fallen as a result of "that deed" which was to liberate him from human constrictions. Of course, in his cardinal shape (boy bishop on the loose) Faustus releases Bruno and returns him to Germany. But by this trick he has simply given the world another pope, and one, too, at whose feet he himself is prepared to lay his life (B.84).

Faustus's second piece of magical sport, putting horns on a knight who is rudely skeptical about his supernatural powers, is a companion piece to the spectacle of Alexander and his paramour with which Faustus entertains the emperor. Here again, there is the retribution theme, but it is connected this time with Faustus's arrogant disbelief rather than his arrogant pride. The theme of retribution is advanced in doubly ironic manner, too. As later at the court of Vanholt, the patronizing promise of reward for magical services rendered ("Expect from me a bounteous reward") brings to mind another promise of requital: "The reward of sin is death" (1.40). The emperor exits as he makes his promise, whereupon Faustus's thoughts are dragged for a few moments out of pastime into time past and time future: "The restless course / That time doth run with calm and silent foot, / Shortening my days and thread of vital life, / Calls for the payment of my latest years" (9.92–95). This does not fully exhaust the ironic parallels in the horning of the skeptical knight. Not only does the incident identify Faustus with Diana, patroness of witchcraft, but it also foreshadows his final degradation, the desire to be "changed / Unto some brutish beast" (13.100–101).

The B-text version of this scene is characteristically both more spectacular and more pointed and inventive in its ironic analogies. It is also closely linked with the B version of the papal scene, and not a discrete episode. The release of Bruno, the emperor's appointee, has made Faustus a hero in the imperial court before he arrives, and his entry is consequently a triumphal one. Like the Alexander show, the humiliation of the knight, now called Benvolio, is correspondingly more elaborate than its counterpart in A. It is more farcical, but it has a heroic dimension, too, for Benvolio seeks retaliation with a band of murderous knights and they are all overwhelmingly defeated—"made the laughing stocks of all the world" (B.91)—by the scholar and his army of drumming, firecracking devils.

Sense, however, is not smothered by spectacle. The emperor makes a manifestly hollow promise of a huge reward (using Faustus's favorite verb): "In recompense of this thy high desert, / Thou shalt command the state of Germany" (B.87). An aspect of the Diana-Actaeon myth ignored by the A text is profitably introduced. After his transformation into a stag by the angry goddess, Actaeon's fate was to be torn apart by her hounds. Just so, Benvolio and Faustus both promise to "recompense this deed" (B.89) with dismemberment. Benvolio is deluded for a while into thinking he succeeds (Faustus's false head is struck off), and Faustus comes as near to success as he wants to. Image and diction here continually foreshadow Faustus's end, when God will recompense him for his deed, when the threat of dismemberment will strip him of all courage and throw him into the arms of "Hellen," and when triumphant devils will mock his "idle fantasies" ("Was this the face that launched a thousand ships?") just as these seemingly triumphant knights mock him before being finally mocked themselves:

Was this that stern aspect, that awful frown
Made the grim monarch of infernal spirits
Tremble and quake at his commanding charms? (B.88–89)

Faustus's third and last piece of magical sport forcefully registers the extent of his spiritual decline, for it brings him down into the clown subplot (Levin, 122), which we must now consider. The clown comedy begins impressively in scene 2 with the encounter between Wagner and two Scholars. The encounter is essentially a contest between gravity and levity, between realistic fear and evasive frivolity. Anxious about their friend's association with Valdes and Cornelius, the Scholars are determined that he should hear "grave counsel" (2.36). For his part, the witty servant dodges their questions about Faustus's whereabouts with "jesting" (2.8) quibbles and with parodies of both logical argumentation and solemn religious language (of the Puritan or "precisian" type). The servant is clearly an imitation of his master, but not until two scenes later can we be certain that the function of such parody is to deflate Faustus rather than to dignify him by contrast. Wagner's scene with the Clown (where he is to the Clown as Mephastophilis is to Faustus) produces vivid and damaging analogies with Faustus's present and future conduct. Here in gross form are Faustus's levity ("See how poverty jesteth in his nakedness" [4.6; cf. 24]), his reckless bargain ("The villain . . . would give his soul to the devil for a shoulder of mutton" [4.7–9]), his claim to heroic fearlessness (4.44–48), and his servile submission to threats of dismemberment (4.50–72). Yet the Clown is, by implication, wiser than Faustus, for he sees that the deal offered by Wagner is a bad one and accepts it only under threat. Wagner, too, it appears, is just as godlike as Faustus, for he has already learned how to make devils obey his behests. Immediately preceding, as it does, the solemn signing of the deed of gift, this scene reduces Faustus's conception of his magical career to the level of a grand illusion even before it begins.

In the two scenes with the stablemen, Robin and Rafe—immediately preceding and following Faustus's sport with the pope—the analogical structure continues, the parallels are varied, and as before, the ironic import is both retrospective and prospective. Having stolen one of Faustus's conjuring books, even Robin can summon Mephastophilis—all the way from Constantinople, too. Robin threatens Rafe with dismemberment and cajoles him into a deal with the promise that he can have Nan Spit, the kitchen maid, to his pleasure ("Was this the face . . . ?"). Together they "gull" the Vintner "supernaturally" (8.6) and steal his goblet, just as Faustus snatched the pope's. For their "apish deeds" (a richly suggestive phrase: devil and witch ape God and make covenants), Robin and Rafe are transformed into an ape and a dog, respectively, by the infuriated Mephastophilis. All this "fine sport" (8.45) is rather tedious (a sense of the repetitive has set in), but one cannot say that it obscures the central significances of the play.

The scene at the Vanholt palace, where Faustus gratifies the Duchess's longing for grapes in the dead of winter, begins with a line that might be interpreted as the attempt of an uneasy playwright to justify the farcical scene that has just ended, the episode of the Horse-courser: "Believe me, master doctor, this merriment hath much pleased me" (11.1–2). Whatever may be said about the taste of Renaissance princes for such things, it is with the jugglery of the Horse-courser scene that the patience of many critics visibly runs out. This may be due in some degree to the fact that Faustus has here descended to the level of playing tricks on yokels. That in itself, as already noted, is significant, a sign of the depths to which the great man has fallen. Everything else is relevant as ironic comment. As in the skeptical-knight episode, Faustus makes a great joke out of what will soon confront him in terrifying earnest, the threat of dismemberment (here it is his leg and not his head that he pretends to lose). He outwits the Horse-courser in an exchange of goods, and this fool is a strikingly exact and unflattering version of himself. As with Faustus and his devil pact, it is the Horse-courser's pestering that initiates the treacherous bargain. More interestingly, "like a ventrous youth," the Horse-courser "would not be ruled" by the injunction not to ride the horse through water, and so ends up seated in midpond on a bottle of hay, "near drowning" (10.33–37). The Icarus parallel is neat and does much to redeem the episode. So does the abrupt, but psychologically right, revelation in the middle of the scene that Faustus is weary and fearful in spirit, perhaps even disgusted with his present life (an impression powerfully communicated in Barry Kyle's 1989 production at Stratford). Picking up on the Horse-courser's initial satisfaction with his bargain, "Now am I a man made for ever" (10.17), he soliloquizes, "What art thou, Faustus, but a man condemned to die? / Thy fatal time doth draw to final end" (10.24–25). This anticipates what Wagner as chorus will say after the next scene: "I think my master means to die shortly . . . belike the feast is ended."

Caring less perhaps for artistic economy than for the tastes of his audience, the author of the B text expands the Horse-courser episode.[5] He also conflates it with that of the Vanholts, thus giving Faustus's playing with the common man a little more dignity, something to amuse their lordships. The scene ends with a comment from the gratified Duke that explains, with penetrating dramatic irony, the significance of Faustus's long feast of folly, placing it unintentionally in the context of eternity and hell. To his wife's gracious remark that "we are much beholding to this learned man," the Duke blandly responds:

> So are we madam, which we will recompense
> With all the love and kindness that we may:
> His artful sport drives all sad thoughts away. (B.100)

Unlike their counterparts in Shakespearean tragedy, the comic scenes in *Doctor Faustus* more often than not leave us with the impression of a play that is aesthetically uneven, but aesthetic unevenness is certainly not conceptual disunity. Close examination of the comic parts discloses a remarkable degree of conceptual control and a system of ironies that not only comments on what has passed but continually points to the end in the spirit of the demon's dry response to one of the hero's jesting evasions of reality: "Ay, think so still, till experience change thy mind" (5.128).

9

Distress

I

At the heart of most great tragedies lies an intense conflict between human aspiration and human limitation. The major instance and symbol of such limitation is death. *Doctor Faustus*, however, because of the story on which it is based and the religious culture and dramatic tradition that inform it, attaches an importance to death that is exceptional, if not unique, in tragedy.

For the moment of death in this narrative is fixed and, if the devil gets his due, the end of life for Faustus will entail the beginning of eternal torment. Death therefore reflects backward to determine the significance of everything else in the play. "Remember thy last end," moreover, was an insistent message in medieval and sixteenth-century Christianity. In devotional literature, this preoccupation occasioned innumerable treatises on "the art of dying," writings that highlight the importance of repentance, the dangers of despair, and the struggle between demons and angels at the final moment for the soul of the dying person. In masques and the visual arts, the same preoccupation gave rise to the Dance of Death, a theme that sardonically represents the whole of human life, with all its ambitions and desires, as a macabre dance led by the grinning specter himself. Tied to an emphasis on the importance of repentance, the imminence of death was a major concern in the morality plays. It is conspicuous, for example, in *The Castle of Perseverance* (1405–25) and *Wisdom* (1460–70), and it dominates *Everyman* (1495), where death is personified and present from the start as the prime mover of the action.

Time is Death's unofficial instrument in *Everyman*, as well as the author's device for structural unity and dramatic suspense. The play opens with Death calling a halt to Everyman's "sport and play" (210, 275).[1] Ignoring his plea to "spare me till to-morrow" (173), Death gives Everyman one day in which to prepare for the final reckoning, when he will be judged, not by his words, but by his deeds alone. The enduring appeal of *Everyman* lies in the ever-increasing sense of "distress" (218, 391, 508) experienced by the once chirpy protagonist as he seeks by one means after another to undo in the very limited time at his disposal the likelihood that he will be "damned indeed" (510) because of his deeds (too many bad, not enough good).

Faustus's career of proud, audacious deeds finds its crucial expression in the deed that he signs with Mephastophilis. As we have seen, the recurrent pun on the word *deed* keeps the covenant in the foreground of our consciousness even when play and sport have helped to suppress it in his. This punning and the attendant structure of theme and action suggest that Marlowe might have known *Everyman*. Be that as it may, the resemblances are worth noting as further evidence of the closeness of Marlowe's tragedy to the morality tradition. The pact story, however, lent itself better to tragic treatment than would the kind of simple structure devised by the *Everyman* author, since it posits a single rash act or commitment with potentially catastrophic consequences and since, as medieval versions of the story demonstrated, it is a natural vehicle for conflicting beliefs about fatality and freedom. In medieval versions, the rash mortal usually wins a last-minute release from a seemingly preordained fate, so that Christian providentialism and belief in freedom of the will and the efficacy of prayer are shown to triumph over fatalistic pagan ideas associated with magic and fostered by Satan. But not always: a few versions give the devil his victim so as to demonstrate the dangers of spiritual rebellion or of despair.[2] The sixteenth century, with its obsessive fears about witchcraft and its Protestant preoccupation with the virtual impotence of the human will in matters spiritual, made the tragic ending its own.

It is arguable that Marlowe conceived of his tragedy as, above all else, an experience of total "distress." In some of his most agonized moments, the protagonist speaks of "distressed Faustus' soul" (5.251, 258) and later—shifting the emphasis a little from the physical to the spiritual—of his "distressed soul" (12.49). In its dramatic context, the word *distressed* is richly complex and economical. Like the *Everyman* author, Marlowe hints at its legal sense: *distress* meaning "the act of distraining [i.e., binding, confining]; the legal seizure and detention of a chattel . . . for the purpose of constraining the owner to pay money owed by him or to make satisfaction for some wrong done by him" (*OED*). Quite simply, therefore, the pun acknowledges that Faustus's distress in the sense of "sorrow, anguish, or affliction" (*OED*) is caused by the fact that he is bound "by articles inviolate" to repay Lucifer with his "body and soul, flesh, blood, or goods" (5.107–9). Marlowe implies a third meaning, one that enables him—characteristically—to fuse word, stage image, and action into an expressive whole. Both the noun and verb forms of *distress* are cognate with the verb *distrain*, which means not only "to constrain, force, or compel" in the legal sense but also (a sense now obsolete) "to rend or tear asunder" (*OED*), coming as it does from the Latin *distringere*, "to draw or tear apart."

It was a commonplace of the witchcraft tradition for the devil to subject his followers to fierce beatings if they wavered in allegiance to him. In *The Damnable Life*, this commonplace takes the form of a repeated threat of dismemberment, but Marlowe, in adapting the motif, has adroitly assimilated it to his own imaginative strategies. The first two uses of the phrase "distressed Faustus' soul" (5.251, 258) are pointedly placed immediately before and after the first threat that if he repents, "devils shall tear thee in pieces" (5.255). In the preceding scene, too, comes the first of the play's comic visualizations of the dismemberment motif: the Clown reluctantly agrees to bind himself to Wagner after devils with "vile long nails" have chased him about the stage as if to "tear" him "in pieces" (4.27, 50). So the repeated warning that Faustus will be torn apart if he tries to renounce the deed by repenting means that he is distressed in a triple sense—profoundly, inescapably distressed, as it were. The image of physical dismemberment in turn provides an emblem for the emotional and spiritual anguish that Faustus's state of entrapment and servitude entails, its psychological significance being spelled out in his final speech when he begs the devil, "Ah, rend not my heart for naming of my Christ" (13.74). We instinctively think of "distress" as a tearing of mind and heart. This condition is magnificently apparent in the last two scenes and some of the early ones as well, but it exists as visual recollection and anticipation in the intervening scenes of clownage, too.

Uncertainty is a primary symptom of Faustus's distress throughout the play, uncertainty first as to whether he should do the deed, but then, and primarily, as to whether he can undo it. This uncertainty proceeds from a "psychomachia," or conflict of spiritual beliefs and forces that are outwardly embodied in the characters of the Good Angel, the Old Man, and the Scholars of the last scene, on the one hand, and, on the other, the Evil Angel, the magicians Cornelius and Valdes, Mephastophilis, and Lucifer. The opening soliloquy, in which Faustus coolly decides to practice necromancy, is promptly followed by the appearance of the Good Angel and the Evil Angel. If we take the standard Christian view of angels, we must assume that these two characters are objective beings, messengers of God and Satan, respectively, whose intervention shows that what Faustus is doing matters greatly to heaven and hell. Only in the B text, however, and there only in the last scene, does Faustus address either of them, and this suggests that they are also (if not only) projections of his mental and spiritual state, voices from within. Thus, although the Good Angel's solemn warning that the "damned book" will incur God's heavy wrath does not deter Faustus, it does indicate that the bravura display of decisiveness is to some extent misleading: a part of him rejects what he is about to do and will in time assert itself more forcefully. Yet, the Evil Angel's speech chimes in so exactly with his own prior reflections that he cannot be seen as the victim of demonic pressure, but must be regarded, rather, as a man whose masterful desires need only a little encouragement to proceed on their preferred path. Just such an idea is specified in his ensuing comments to Valdes and Cornelius: "Not your words only [have won me to magic], but mine own fantasy, / That will receive no object for my head, / But ruminates on necromantic skill" (1.103–5).

Distress proper begins and figures at several points in the long scene (virtually the whole of act 2 in the conjectural five-act division) where Faustus signs the deed. Having already conjured the devil and blasphemously abjured God, Faustus knows that he has made what theologians called an "implicit pact" with hell and that signing the deed will merely formalize his new situation. Thus, the intense conflict between despair and hope that will torment him to the last commences even before Mephastophilis arrives with the document. Faustus wavers between inner and outer voices, which tell him both that damnation *is* now necessary and inevitable, and that it is *not*, that contrition, prayer, and repentance will save him, and that these things are lunatic illusions (5.1–20). Although Faustus gives in to the Evil Angel's advice to "think of honour and of wealth" (5.21), he does so less because such thoughts are overwhelmingly attractive at this point than because they serve as anodynes for despair. This is made clear when the conflict erupts for the second time. When Faustus declares (with the Good Angel's support) that God will pity him if he repents, the Evil Angel responds with demoralizing assurance, "Ay, but Faustus never shall repent," and then confidently departs. This brings from Faustus the miserable revelation that he has tried many times to pray and repent and that "long ere this I should have slain myself, / Had not sweet pleasure conquered deep despair" (5.177–210). Yet, the forces of hell are by no means calmly confident when the next crisis occurs: Faustus manages a fervent prayer—"Ah Christ, my Saviour, seek to save / Distressed Faustus' soul"—which has to be neutralized by the threat of dismemberment, the terrifying intervention of Lucifer, and devilish pastimes.

In the last scene, Faustus reveals to his friends that he has often thought of seeking spiritual aid, but that "the devil threatened to tear me in pieces if I named God" (13.43–46). Constant repetition of the psychomachic conflict would have been theatrically ineffectual, but this revelation indicates that during the long interval of artful sport nothing changed fundamentally. Appropriately, however, the psychomachia is openly renewed by the response of an outraged but sorrowful Old Man (a version of the morality agent of repentance)[3] to Faustus's most ambitious performance, the showing of Helen. The compassionate humanity that invests the Old Man's appeal for repentance gives to this version of the familiar crisis a new intensity, for if Faustus is further than ever from righteousness and mercy, he also feels nearer: "Ah, my sweet friend, I feel thy words / To comfort my distressed soul." In the event, this proximity merely adds to his distress ("Accursed Faustus, where is mercy now? / I do repent, and yet I do despair: / Hell strives with grace for conquest in my breast") and brings on him the wrath of Mephastophilis ("Revolt, or I'll in piecemeal tear thy flesh"). The acuteness of Faustus's distress is strangely enhanced here by the unheroic vindictiveness with which he turns against the Old Man for feeding him with futile hopes: "Torment . . . that base and crooked age . . . With greatest torments that our hell affords" (12.44–67).

One remarkable aspect of the great final scene is that Faustus enters in a mood of calm and total despair ("The serpent that tempted Eve may be saved, but not Faustus"), only to be tormented again, and to the last, by hope—prompted now by the words of his scholar friends ("Remember, God's mercies are infinite!") and fed by his vision of Christ's blood streaming in the firmament and by other, more desperate imaginings. Another reason for the extraordinary power of this conclusion is the fact that the forces that condemn, constrain, menace, and tear at him are all—except for time and the clock—internalized, perceived only by himself, and in consequence newly mysterious:

> Ah my God—I would weep, but the devil draws in my tears! gush forth blood instead of tears . . . O, he stays my tongue! I would lift up my hands, but see, they hold them, they hold them, they hold them!

O I'll leap up to my God! Who pulls me down?
See, see where Christ's blood streams in the firmament!
One drop would save my soul, half a drop: ah my Christ—
Ah, rend not my heart for naming of my Christ;
Yet will I call on him—O spare me Lucifer!
Where is it now? 'Tis gone: and see where God
Stretcheth out his arm, and bends his ireful brows! (13.71–77)

My God, my God, look not so fierce on me! (13.112)

When the devils enter to seize Faustus, is it because they have won or because he has surrendered? Because God has condemned him, or because he has condemned himself?

II

The consummation of Faustus's anguish coincides with the striking of the midnight bell. As with Everyman, but in a much more complex manner, time is fundamental to Faustus's experience of distress. There are two mutually supportive conceptions of time at work in the play, the biblical and the cosmological: both stand for the limiting, finite order against which Faustus rebels in vain. In the biblical conception, time is a precious gift, not to be wasted, but to be used for securing the soul's salvation in eternity. A key text, echoed repeatedly throughout *Doctor Faustus*, is Luke 12.19–20: "And I will say to my soule, Soule, thou hast muche goods laid up for many years: live at ease, eate, drinke, and take thy pastime. But God said unto him, O foole, this night will they fetch away thy soule from thee." In the cosmological conception (briefly referred to in chapter 6), time is nature seen as a dynamic, mobile order. It is also, as Plato said, a moving image of eternity, so that to study the stars, the determinants of time, is to arrive at "an understanding of our relationship to the deity and to his handmaid nature" (Heninger, 12–13). As summary analysis will reveal, these two concepts are continuously present in the play, often investing the most trivial situations and exchanges with central significance.

The opening soliloquy shows that Faustus's attraction to necromancy is motivated to a large extent by a sense of human limitation conceived in terms of time and mortality. He is dissatisfied with medicine because it enables him to save lives but does not allow him to "make men to live eternally, / Or, being dead, raise them to life again" (1.24–25). Theology is even less acceptable because it teaches that we die as a consequence of original sin, and "die an everlasting death" because of present sins (1.44–46). Thus, Faustus opts for necromancy, so named because it seeks to raise the dead, and then he blots out the thought of eternity in exchange for "four and twenty years" of living "in all voluptuousness" (3.92–93). The choice of "twenty four" is ironically appropriate, for his interval of pagan pseudodivinity will in the end seem no more than a day. The biblical warning note is struck in the next scene when Wagner threatens the Clown: "Why, now, sirra, thou art at an hour's warning whensoever or wheresoever the devil will fetch thee," the effective word being St. Luke's "fetch" (4.35–36).

Faustus's dialogue with Mephastophilis in the following scene on the "motions and dispositions" of the planets (5.168) elicits relevant truths on the subject of time. The planets may be "erring stars," but they are nonetheless part of a spatio-temporal order, "having all one motion, both *situ et tempore* [in place and time]." They have a "double motion," too, "the first finished in a natural day, the second thus: as Saturn in thirty years; Jupiter in twelve; Mars in four; the Sun, Venus, and Mercury in a year; the Moon in twenty-eight days" (5.219–31). Erring star of Wittenberg and would-be defier of divinely ordained natural limits, Faustus dismisses all this as boringly familiar. Evidently, however, it has affected him subconsciously, for he is soon asking about the Creator and agonizing over whether it is "too late" or "never too late" to repent (5.252–54). He is deflected from this inquiry by threats and "pastime," and so fails to catch the frisson of terror in Lucifer's departing promise to show him more delights in hell: "I will send for thee at midnight" (5.274, 340).

Faustus's aerial journeys "to know the secrets of astronomy / Graven in the book of Jove's high firmament" are essentially fruitless. So, too, is his Italian journey: he "spent his time" admiring the kind of church "that threats the stars with her aspiring tops" (chor.2.2,

7.19–20). He also found no special significance in the "castle passing strong" protected by 365 brass cannons, which "match the days within one complete year" (2.36–40). The B text draws attention to the dangerously time-wasting nature of the sports that follow. Faustus's promise here, "My four and twenty years of liberty / I'll spend in pleasure and in dalliance," is obliquely answered by the pope's comment on the chained Bruno: "Thus as the gods creep on with feet of wool, / Long ere with iron hands they punish men, / So shall our sleeping vengeance now arise, / And smite with death thy hated enterprise" (B.72–73).

At the emperor's court, Faustus at last seems to raise the dead "from hollow vaults below," and in the shapes and attire "they used to wear during their time of life" (9.31, 35). He has to admit, however, that the bodies are "consumed to dust" (9.44), so the emperor's departure leaves him in somber mood. He must "make haste to Wittenberg," since "the restless course / That time doth run with calm and silent foot, / Shortening my days and thread of vital life, / Calls for the payment of my latest years" (9.93–96). The same somber mood sours the Horse-courser scene: "What art thou Faustus, but a man condemned to die? / Thy fatal time doth draw to final end" (10.5–6). The Vanholt episode, however, presents an entirely cheerful attempt to defy time's limiting order: grapes for the Duchess in "the dead time of winter." How is it done? Faustus explains (and we must forget about refrigerated containers) that "the year is divided into two circles over the whole world, that when it is here winter with us, in the contrary circle it is summer with them, as in India . . . and by means of a swift spirit that I have, I had brought them hither" (11.19–23). Chorus 4 tells of Faustus's desperate carousals with students in the attempt to forget that "the feast is ended." Then there is terrified despair after the Old Man's first visit: "Hell calls for right . . . thine hour is come" (12.40–41); the embrace of Helen is a fleeting escape from time ("Make me immortal with a kiss"); and in the last scene Time, functioning as the iron hand of divine retribution, takes hold of Faustus and encloses him within the narrow confines of his magic circle: "The date is expired, the time will come, and he will fetch me" (13.40).

Emerging as it does from this context, the verbal and nonverbal language of the last soliloquy is stunningly powerful and meaningful. Like that enduring castle with its 365 cannons, the speech itself matches time's order: the clock strikes at eleven, at half-past eleven, and at midnight; at half-past the hour Faustus has spoken 30 lines. The speech presents, too, through the agonized consciousness of the astrologer, a vast, complex, limiting order that will not yield to his desires and commands. The supreme irony of the play's ending is that Faustus learns—"too late"—that those who despise the ends and limits of human knowledge and of nature are rewarded in kind. "Hell hath no limits" (5.121), Mephastophilis explained once. Now Faustus laments, "O, no end is limited to damned souls," and begs, in those lines of ultimate distress, for "some end to my incessant pain" (13.93–96). The playwright's concluding motto is most apt: "The hour ends the day, the author ends his work." It recalls the grave inscriptions found on many sundials in the sixteenth century—reminders of time passing, of time's order, and of eternity.[4]

III

Faustus's agony on the rack of terrified despair was an essentially Christian experience that had strong roots in the past but was especially characteristic of the Reformation period. As I have already indicated, medieval versions of the pact story were used as lessons against despair, exemplifying the point that contrition and humble prayer can liberate the soul from seemingly impossible straits. Devil-induced despair was the last great threat to the soul in the arts-of-dying treatises. In the moralities, despair was seen as a greater danger to the mankind figure than his initial fall into sin. But no period in Christian history records the dangers and terrors of religious despair so often or with such conviction as the Reformation: "Imagine what thou canst," wrote Robert Burton in his *Anatomie of Melancholy* (1621), "fear, sorrow, furies, grief, pain, terror, anger, dismal, ghastly . . . it is not sufficient, it comes far short [of religious despair]. . . . 'Tis an epitome of hell, an extract, a quintessence, a compound, a mixture of all feral [fierce] maladies, tyrannical tortures, plagues and perplexities."[5]

One general reason for this obsession with despair was the breakup of Christianity into two sects, each of which condemned the other in endless polemics of Satanic error and wickedness. John Donne and Ben Jonson, who changed from one faith to the other, must have been two among many who were troubled by the possibility that they had risked damnation by making the wrong choice. A more particular reason for the prevalence of religious despair was Protestant teaching on justification by faith and on predestination. The first of these doctrines deprived the believer of the assurance that good works could in some degree contribute to the saving of one's soul: salvation was ascribed entirely to faith in the unmerited grace of God as won by Christ's death. Afflicted by a sense of their own sinfulness, many good Protestants found it difficult to remain confident that such grace would be extended to them. For many, these doubts and fears were increased tremendously by the doctrine of predestination, especially in its extreme Calvinist form as reprobation. Catholics and moderate Anglicans held that those who were saved were predestined by God to be saved, and that the rest were damned in consequence of their own sinfulness, but Calvin taught that the rest were predestined by their Creator for damnation and that no efforts on their part could alter that "horrible decree" (as he himself termed it).

The religious conditions of the time thus gave rise to a great deal of anguished self-scrutiny, examination of conscience (thought of as the condemning or approving voice of God) to determine whether one was in the state of grace or even whether one belonged to the elect rather than the reprobate. And so, from about 1580 to 1630, there issued from the press a stream of treatises and individual case histories on conscience, showing "how a man may know whether he be a Child of God or no," offering "reliefe of such as are afflicted in Conscience," or providing "Instruction and Comfort of such as are distressed in Conscience."[6] By far the most famous case history from the period is that of Francis Spira, the Italian Protestant who recanted under pressure from the Inquisition, fell into despair, became convinced that he was reprobate, attempted suicide, and died soon afterward. Spira's case was clumsily dramatized in the form of a morality play in Nathaniel Woode's *Conflict of Conscience* (1581). Marlowe may have known this play, and he must surely have heard about Spira, the age's archetype of religious wavering and despair (Campbell, 219–29). At any rate, it is clear that *Doctor Faustus* is even more deeply embedded in contemporary culture than critical concentration on the subject of witchcraft and the Renaissance theme of superhuman power and knowledge would allow us to believe.

Marlowe dramatized Faustus's psychic torment in a manner that moves audiences in every period and culture profoundly, for wisdom that comes too late, desperate regrets, feelings of total entrapment, despair, and terror are experiences we can all empathize with. Faustus's distress, however, has a problematic character that demands consideration in the light of its historical-religious context. Ostensibly, its theological implications are fairly clear and simple. Faustus has sinned not lightly or impulsively but gravely and with total deliberation. Not only has he disobeyed God, he has elaborately defied and mocked him. Since Faustus knows very well the extent of his sin, his belief in the possibility of forgiveness is necessarily fragile. His continued persistence in sin enfeebles his faith still further—or as he himself puts it, in standard theological terms, it hardens his heart against the offer of God's mercy (5.194).

Thus, although Faustus would like to repent, he cannot bring himself to do so properly. His periodic acceptance of the devil's claim that the deed is a legally binding contract, from which he cannot escape and which even Christ, because "he is just" (5.259), must respect, is simply despair rationalized and certainly mistaken. It was common knowledge that oaths and covenants "which do promise evil and unlawful things" are not binding; to respect them was judged a "double offence" against God.[7] It was also well known that in his manipulation of the pact, the devil "feints, cunning as he is, to work under necessity, yet all the time it is really voluntarily."[8] The devils in *Doctor Faustus* clearly believe that the deed is not binding and that the possibility of Faustus obtaining divine forgiveness is no illusion. Otherwise they would not terrorize and distract him every time he thinks of repentance. Faustus's abject surrender to their threats, too, is not just an ironic comment on his heroic self-conception but also, and more important, a symptom of his despair: if he truly believed in God's power to forgive him, then he would have the strength to resist. This is made clear in the response of Mephastophilis to his request that the Old Man be tormented for urging him to renege on the deed. "His faith is great, I cannot touch his soul, / But what I may afflict his body with, / I will attempt—which is but little worth" (12.66–71).

Although despair was seen as the consequence of sin and a sin in itself (a form of pride), it is precisely the kind of spiritual malady that is most likely to provoke pity in the observer rather than censure. Coupled with his admissions of guilt, his repeated attempts to repent, and his subjection to demonic terrorizing, Faustus's failure to muster true faith in God's mercy strikes us much more as an affliction than a culpable condition. In the end, therefore, a sense of cruel fatality hangs over this tragedy whose hero originally seemed so clearly responsible for what happens to him. For those in Marlowe's audience who held to the Calvinist doctrine of reprobation, this paradox would have been easily resolved: since Faustus is clearly damned in the end, he was necessarily predestined to be so, and all his spiritual and moral flaws and all his failed efforts to repent were simply the acting-out of that unchangeable decree—fate is character. A number of critics have in fact argued that Marlowe consciously presented Faustus as the victim of reprobation, either because Marlowe was imaginatively committed to that doctrine when he wrote the play or because he wished to subvert Calvinist theology by emphasizing its cruelty, thus presenting a profoundly heterodox play in the guise of orthodoxy.

Over and above the final impression of a cruel fatality, specific textual evidence in support of the predestinarian interpretation has been adduced. Much, for example, has been made of the word *conspire* in the opening chorus, most recently by John Stachniewski. Quoting the chorus as follows,

> And melting heavens conspirde his overthrow.
> For falling to a divelish exercise . . .
> He surfetts upon cursed Negromancy . . .
> Which he preferres before his chiefest bliss,

Stachniewski claims that these lines rehearse, in correct order, the causal process that leads to Faustus's damnation: "God first conspires by means of predestinarian decrees"; the devil, as permitted by God, "plays an active manipulative part" in the conspiracy; and "lastly there is a concurrence of the human will, chiming in with antecedent necessity."[9] This argument loses its force, however, if one views the context and the appropriate dictionary. The first line quoted above is immediately preceded in the same sentence by "Till, swollen with cunning, of a self-conceit, / His waxen wings did mount above his reach." Read thus, the causal process is, first, the sin of Icarian pride and, then, divine punishment for that sin. (Since Faustus later identifies his "cunning" with necromancy—"I gave them my soul for my cunning" [13.35]—Marlowe would already seem to be identifying Icarian pride specifically with the cursed art.) To the modern reader, however, the word *conspired* still seems disturbing, deliberately so. The obvious choice for Marlowe would have been some such term as *caused* or *effected*. For us, the chosen word has no such neutral connotation but carries rather a single, sinister sense that seems to warrant inverting the causal sequence defined by the syntax and to postulate a prior malicious determination on the part of the heavens to bring Faustus down. Marlowe, however, would have known that the etymological meaning of the word is "to breathe or blow together" (Latin, *con-spirare*), and he would many times have seen the word used in the neutral or laudatory sense of "to combine in action or aim; to act in purposive combination, union, or harmony" (*OED*), as in "the cyvyle life ys a polytyke ordur of men conspyryng togeyddur in vertue and honesty" (Starkey, 1538). It would seem therefore that Marlowe, having this sense in mind, chose the word simply because it was metrically right. (With the etymological sense in mind, too, he may also have thought it especially appropriate in describing the reaction of "the heavens"—Nature/God—to an overambitious high-flier: sun and wind combine to sink him.)

A more cogent piece of textual evidence adduced in favor of the predestinarian thesis is the fact that Faustus's first prayer for divine help is immediately answered by the appearance of an outraged, demonic trinity (5.258ff.). A strict Calvinist would certainly have interpreted this as showing that God had abandoned Faustus to the devils, but a moderate Anglican or a Catholic might have seen this brilliantly theatrical incident as a test of faith, the kind to which the Old Man is subjected at the end, when no angel intervenes to protect him from a demonic onslaught (12.104–9). Also cited in support of this argument is Mephastophilis's claim in the B text that it was he who led Faustus's eye into misreading the Bible, and so robbed him of eternal happiness. Even if this claim were inconsistent with the initial impression of a willful choice, one could ascribe it largely to the B text's enthusiasm for the ocular motif rather than to any change of theological perspective. But I do not think it is inconsistent. Throughout, the devils have been leading Faustus's eye in the direction it was pleased to go. Misinterpretation of the Bible was a mode of temptation frequently ascribed to them, and no less typical of them was a habit of gloating triumphantly over their victims. It would be entirely in character for them to take full credit for the downfall of a sinner, ignoring the fact that their role was only a contributory one.

A serious weakness in the predestinarian thesis is that nowhere in the play is the idea of reprobation specified, either by the devils or (as in *The Conflict of Conscience*) by the protagonist. It is not even thrust in as a notion to be dismissed by the Good Angel or the Old Man. There is no reason whatever why Marlowe should have been so shy about alluding to a doctrine that was allegedly so important to him. The one fatalistic belief specified is that of astrological determinism. In his last speech Faustus says that the influence of the stars "allotted death and hell" (13.84). But that was a discredited pagan belief that no one in Marlowe's audience would have taken seriously. Besides, Faustus goes on to blame his parents, and then himself, and then Lucifer, for his fate, which suggests that the question of tragic causality admits of no simple answer.

The argument that Marlowe gave ironic allegiance to the grim doctrine of reprobation in *Doctor Faustus* and, in so doing, produced a heterodox, subversive play is unconvincing for several reasons.[10] The totally inaudible, inexplicit nature of this "irony" in a play so overtly ironical in all other respects makes its existence hard to accept. Even if one grants that it does exist, it does not follow that *Doctor*

Faustus is a heterodox, subversive play from the point of view of the official teaching of the established church. Article 17, "Of Predestination and Election," in the Thirty-nine Articles speaks of "predestination to life" and enthuses on the "sweet, pleasant, and unspeakable comfort" that this doctrine brings to godly persons who feel in themselves the working of Christ. It has nothing to say about those who are not saved; whether they are predestined for damnation or are damned because they abuse free will and prevenient grace is left for readers to decide for themselves.[11] In the 1590s, however, the more Calvinistic members of the church made great efforts to have this politic ambiguity removed. Their efforts culminated in the so-called Lambeth Articles of 1595. However, the queen and her chief secretary, Lord Burghley, "misliked much" the harsh and contentious nature of the new pronouncements on predestination, and in consequence, publication of the Lambeth Articles was not permitted; they were not even presented to convocation. Thus, although the Calvinists themselves had chosen somewhat presumptuously to describe the doctrines enshrined in these articles as "orthodoxal" and although in this they had the support of the Archbishop of Canterbury and the Bishop of London (as well as the ardently Calvinistic divines in Cambridge), the new articles never achieved official confirmation in the teaching of the Church of England. In short, the ultra-Calvinistic attempt to hijack English orthodoxy failed.[12] To contend, therefore, that Marlowe was tilting at the doctrine of reprobation in *Doctor Faustus* is to make him a defender of the faith as upheld by queen and state—hardly a theological subversive, and certainly not a political one.

Having said this, however, one must also acknowledge that Faustus's repeated failures to win God's mercy do communicate the sense of a cruel fatality and that the whole Christian concept of eternal damnation is exposed by Marlowe in all its horror. If Marlowe was tilting at anything, it was at the harshness of Christian theology itself, especially as exaggerated by the Reformation emphasis on human weakness and corruption. Perhaps, too—though this is a more speculative point—he was tilting at the ruthlessness of a state that could torture and execute any who would not conform to its notion of a "moderate" Christianity. To go beyond that and argue that Marlowe was implicitly rejecting either the doctrine of reprobation or Christian teaching, as such, is, I am sure, mistaken. Marlowe committed himself, with all his imagination, to the basic spiritual outlook of the given story, whether because it provided the basis of a theatrically powerful parable on the subject of human aspiration and limitation or because it articulated his own present or past spiritual terrors, or both.

Perhaps the most important objection to the predestinarian thesis is that it is reductive. It simplifies the tantalizingly complex vision of a play that, like most great tragedy, accommodates two polar perceptions, to neither of which it can be reduced: that the hero suffers because of his own choices and failings, and that he is the victim of a malign destiny. Insofar as a resolution of the tragic paradox of freedom and determination can be discovered in *Doctor Faustus*, it lies in the idea that once the willful deed has been done, the consequences add up to a dynamic that, given the nature of Faustus and the universe he inhabits, takes on the character of an inescapable doom. In critical history, however, Faustus joins Oedipus and many another hero whose tragedy has been so subtly presented by the playwright that one distinguished scholar will unhesitantly ascribe his fall to his character, while another, equally distinguished, will no less unhesitantly ascribe it to the gods.[13]

IV

The ironic echoes of Faustus's early claims and pretensions that persist in the Helen speech and in the final soliloquy are counterbalanced in the concluding scenes by a powerful movement of compassion and respect. "Ay, think so still, till experience change thy mind" (5.128), said Mephastophilis, and experience has indeed changed Faustus. He has acquired dignity and passed from self-deception to self-honesty, from arrogance to modesty, from egoism to fellow feeling. The change has been anticipated in his gracious (albeit subservient) relations with the emperor and the Vanholts, and in the sad soliloquy "What art thou Faustus but a man condemned to die?" It is evident at the last in his generosity to Wagner, in his concern for the safety of his friends, and in his plain admission that "a surfeit of deadly sin . . . hath damned both body and soul" (13.11–12). Even Faustus's despair has a note of remorseless honesty that contrasts most favorably with the specious fatalism of the opening soliloquy. The choric epilogue has been found inadequate in its moralizing exhortation not to emulate "forward wits" (choruses, speaking for ordinary men and women, customarily speak thus). But it strikes the right—the tragic—note when it says:

> Cut is the branch that might have grown full straight,
> And burned is Apollo's laurel bough,
> That sometime grew within this learned man.
> Faustus is gone!

Notes and References

Chapter 3

1. William Hazlitt, in *Marlowe: "Doctor Faustus": A Casebook*, ed. John Jump (London: Macmillan, 1969), 27–28; hereafter cited in the text as *MDF*.

2. A. C. Swinburne, in *Marlowe: The Critical Heritage, 1588–1896*, ed. Millar Maclure (London: Routledge, 1979), 178; hereafter cited in the text as *MCH*.

3. J. A. Symonds, in *Shakespeare's Predecessors in the Drama* (London: Unwin, 1984), 606–14, 631–33.

4. Una Ellis-Fermor, *Christopher Marlowe* (London: Methuen, 1927), 66, 76, 80–81.

5. Leo Kirschbaum, "Marlowe's *Faustus*: A Reconsideration," *Review of English Studies* 19 (1943): 225–41.

6. F. P. Wilson, *Marlowe and the Early Shakespeare* (Oxford: Clarendon Press, 1953), 82–83.

7. Lily B. Campbell, "*Doctor Faustus*: A Case of Conscience," *Publications of the Modern Language Association of America* 67 (1952): 219–39.

8. David Bevington, *From "Mankind" to Marlowe* (Cambridge, Mass.: Harvard University Press, 1962), 252–60.

9. Douglas Cole, *Suffering and Evil in the Plays of Shakespeare* (Princeton, N.J.: Princeton University Press, 1962), 231–42.

10. Harry Levin, *The Overreacher: A Study of Christopher Marlowe* (Cambridge, Mass.: Harvard University Press, 1952), 129, 158.

11. Robert Ornstein, "Marlowe and God: The Tragic Theology of Dr. Faustus," *Publications of the Modern Language Association of America* 83 (1968): 1378–85.

115

12. J. B. Steane, *Marlowe: A Critical Study* (Cambridge: Cambridge University Press, 1964), 158–65; Wilbur Sanders, *The Dramatist and the Received Idea* (Cambridge: Cambridge University Press, 1968), 209, 211, 222–23, 233; herafter cited as Sanders.

13. Una Ellis-Fermor, "The Equilibrium of Tragedy," in *The Frontiers of Drama* (London: Methuen, 1945), 128–30, 140–43.

14. Stephen Greenblatt, *Renaissance Self-Fashioning: From More to Shakespeare* (Chicago and London: Chicago University Press, 1980), 3, 209, 255–59. For Greenblatt's early debt to Foucault, see the autobiographical note in *Learning to Curse: Essays in Early Modern Culture* (London: Routledge, 1990), 3.

15. Jonathan Dollimore, *Radical Tragedy: Religion, Ideology and Power in the Drama of Shakespeare and His Contemporaries* (Brighton: Harvester Press, 1984), 1–2, 89, 106–19.

16. See, for example, William Tydeman, *"Doctor Faustus": Text and Performance* (London: Macmillan, 1984).

Chapter 4

1. *The History of the Damnable Life and Deserved Death of Doctor John Faustus,1592*, modernized and edited by William Rose (London: Routledge; New York: Dutton, n.d.), 65–66; see also p. 89.

2. M. C. Bradbrook, *Themes and Conventions of Elizabethan Tragedy* (Cambridge: Cambridge University Press, 1935), 153.

3. I now adopt the A-text spelling of the demon's name.

4. Editorial attitudes toward the provision of act and scene divisions have varied. There are no act divisions in the composite-text edition by John D. Jump (London: Methuen, 1962), and neither act nor scene division in the A-text edition by David Ormerod and Christopher Wortham (Nedlands, Western Australia: University of Western Australia Press, 1985). Five-act and scene divisions are provided in Michael Keefer's edition of the A text (Peterborough, Ontario: Broadview Press, 1991) and in the David Bevington and Eric Rasmussen edition of the A and the B texts (Manchester: Manchester University Press, 1993). George Hunter was the first to argue that five-act division was authorially intended: see "Five-Act Structure in *Doctor Faustus*," in his *Dramatic Identities and Cultural Tradition: Studies in Shakespeare and His Contemporaries* (Liverpool: Liverpool University Press, 1978, 335–49; repr. from *Tulane Drama Review* 8 (1964).

5. See Willard Farnham, *The Medieval Inheritance of Elizabethan Tragedy* (Oxford: Blackwell, 1936); Frederick Kiefer, *Fortune and Elizabethan Tragedy* (San Marino, Calif.: Huntington Library, 1983).

6. The Lucifer and Adam analogies are in *The Damnable Life* (90–91),

which points out that Lucifer's malevolence has been behind every spiritual and moral disaster in human history from those of Adam and Cain onward.

7. On the contribution of popular tradition to *The Damnable Life* (chapbook collections of magical pranks such as those of Eulenspiegel), see J. W. Smeed, *Faust in Literature* (London: Oxford University Press, 1975), ch. 6.

8. See G. C. Sedgwick, *Of Irony, Especially in Drama* (Toronto: Toronto University Press, 1935); Bert O. States, *Irony and Drama: A Poetics* (Ithaca, N.Y.: Cornell University Press, 1971).

9. R. B. Sewall, *The Vision of Tragedy* (New Haven: Yale University Press, 1959), 66.

Chapter 5

1. Reginald Scot, *The Discoverie of Witchcraft*, ed. Montague Summers (London: Rodker, 1930), 1–41.

2. See, for example, Exodus 7–9, Numbers 24.1–2. Cf. Revelation. 9.20–21

3. See Tertullian, *On Idolatry*, chs. 4, 9–10, and *Apologeticus*, 10–11, 22–24, in *The Writings of Tertullian*, Ante-Nicene Christian Library, ed. Alexander Roberts and James Donaldson (Edinburgh: Clark, 1869), vol. 6; Augustine, *The City of God*, 7.18, 8.19.

4. Jakob Sprenger and Heinrich Kramer, *Malleus Malificarum*, trans. and ed. Montague Summers (London: Rodker, 1928), 18. First published in 1486, this became an authoritative work on witchcraft both for Catholics and Protestants; there were many sixteenth-century editions.

5. Allen G. Debus, *Man and Nature in the Renaissance*, Cambridge History of Science (Cambridge: Cambridge University Press, 1978), 12.

6. D. P. Walker, *Spiritual and Demonic Magic from Ficino to Campanella* (London: Warburg Institute, 1958), 146–47.

7. Frances A. Yates, *The Occult Philosophy in the Elizabethan Age* (London: Routledge, 1979), 37–38, 79–93.

8. It is important to note the A-text spelling *negromantic*, changed by Roma Gill (and other modern editors) to *necromantic*. *Necromancy* means divination by means of the dead (in Greek, *nekros*, "a corpse or dead person"; *manteia*, "divination"), but the word came to denote black magic in general through confusion with the Latin *niger*, meaning "black." It was spelt *negromancy* throughout the Middle Ages. The etymological spelling began to be restored in the sixteenth century, but Marlowe, it would seem, pointedly ignores this.

9. *Malleus Maleficarum*, 20–21, 41, 61–64, 99–100, 104–14, 122–24, 140–43, 227; H. C. Lea, *Materials Towards a History of Witchcraft*, ed. A. C. Howard, 3 vols. (New York and London: Thomas Yoseloff, 1957), 126, 135,

145–62, 193, 199–201, 353, 357–58,4 00. See Scot, *Discoverie of Witchcraft,* 40–41, 51–59, where most of these beliefs are ridiculed.

10. Lea, *Materials,* 190, 191, 194, 198, 213, 276–77, 291, 357; *Malleus,* 3.

11. For documentation on the history of the lust-witchcraft-idolatry equation, see my article "Classical Mythology and Christian Tradition in Marlowe's *Doctor Faustus," Publications of the Modern Language Association of America* 81 (1966): 214–23. Pertinent also is this passage in the *Malleus:* "And in honour of him [Janus, god of the new year], or rather of the devil in the form of that idol, the Pagans made boisterous revelry, and were very merry among themselves, holding dances and feasts. . . . And now bad Christians imitate these corruptions, turning them to lasciviousness when they run about at the time of Carnival with masks and jests and other superstitions. Similarly witches use these revelries of the devil for their own advantage, and work their spells about the time of the New Year in respect of the Divine Offices and Worship; as on St. Andrew's Day and at Christmas" (116).

12. See Sir Philip Sidney, *The Apologie for Poetry,* ed. Geoffrey Shepherd (London: Nelson, 1965), 118, 189–90; J. V. Cunningham, *Woe or Wonder: The Emotional Effect of Shakespearean Tragedy* (Denver, Colo.: University of Colorado Press, 1951), ch. 2. On the tragic hero becoming "his own antithesis," see Maynard Mack, "The Jacobean Shakespeare: Some Observations on the Construction of the Tragedies," in *Jacobean Shakespeare,* Stratford-Upon-Avon Studies 1, ed. Bernard Harris and John Russell Brown (London: Arnold, 1960); T. McAlindon, *English Renaissance Tragedy* (London: Macmillan, 1986), 13–16.

Chapter 6

1. Douglas Cole has noted the prominence of inversion in the ironic patterning of the play in his *Suffering and Evil in the Plays of Christopher Marlowe* (Princeton, N.J.: Princeton University Press, 1962), 220–21. On the Feast of Fools and the Boy Bishop, see E. K. Chambers, *The Medieval Stage,* vol. 1 (Oxford: Clarendon Press, 1903), 274–371; Mikhail Bakhtin, *Rabelais and His World* (1965), trans. Helene Iswolsky (Cambridge, Mass., and London: MIT Press, 1968), 74–82. On inversion as the structuring principle in these festivities, see Chambers, vol. 1, 325–26, Bakhtin, 83–84, and Robert Weimann, *Shakespeare and the Popular Tradition in the Theater* (Baltimore: Johns Hopkins University Press, 1978), 6, 13, 20. On the inversion motif in demonology as part of a language conventionally employed in the Renaissance to establish and condemn the properties of a disorderly world, see Stuart Clark, "Inversion, Misrule and Witchcraft," *Past and Present* 87 (1980): 98–127.

2. "Deo odibile et daemonibus amabile": Bishop Grosseteste of Lincoln (1236), cited in Chambers, *Medieval Stage*, vol. 1, 322.

3. C. L. Barber, "The Form of Faustus' Fortunes Good or Bad," *Tulane Drama Review* 8 (1964): 92–119.

4. See Peter Burke, *Popular Culture in Early Modern Europe* (London: Temple Smith, 1978), ch. 7.

5. See my *Shakespeare's Tragic Cosmos* (Cambridge and New York: Cambridge University Press, 1991), 200–208. Shakespearean citations are from *The Complete Works*, ed. Stanley Wells, Gary Taylor, John Jowett, and William Montgomery (Oxford: Clarendon Press, 1988).

6. Tatian, *Oratio ad Graecos*, ch. 9, in J. P. Migne, *Patrologia Graeca*, vol. 6, 826; *The Sermons of Edwin Sandys, DD* [d. 1587], ed. J. Ayre, Parker Society Publications (Cambridge: Parker Society, 1842), 362.

7. Pierre de la Primaudaye, *Third Volume of the French Academie*, trans. R. Dolman (London, 1601), A2; quoted in S. K. Heninger, Jr., *The Cosmographical Glass: Renaissance Diagrams of the Universe* (San Marino, Calif.: Huntington Library, 1977), 11. Heninger discusses the biblical and cosmological theme of "looking upward" on pp. 9–12.

8. "When I Behold the Heavens: A Reading of *Doctor Faustus*," *English Studies* 67 (1986): 505. By taking account of the biblical and cosmological tradition of "beholding the heavens," my own approach expands and modifies Wymer's interpretation, to which I am much indebted for drawing attention to this imagistic motif in the play.

Chapter 7

1. Jacques Derrida, *Writing and Difference*, trans. Alan Bass (London and Henley: Routledge, 1978), 292 (Derrida's italics).

2. Simon Shepherd, *Marlowe and the Politics of Elizabethan Theatre* (Brighton: Harvester, 1986), 95.

3. Roger Sales, *Christopher Marlowe* (London: Macmillan, 1991), chs. 1, 2, and 7.

4. My argument here is developed from ideas I have already advanced in my article on Faustus in *PMLA* (see ch. 5, n. 11); in "The Ironic Vision: Diction and Theme in Marlowe's *Doctor Faustus*," *Review of English Studies* 32 (1981): 129–41; and in *English Renaissance Tragedy*.

5. "Ludam scilicet illudar [I would play in order, of course, to be deceived/mocked]," warns St. Bernard of Clairvaux, referring to sin and temptation (*Epistola* 87.12, in *Patrologia Latina*, ed. J. P. Migne, vol. 182, 217). See also Migne, vol. 49, 516, 529, 749, 777; vol. 75, 827; vol. 76, 670–71; vol. 83, 664, 668. Compare the *Ancrene Riwle*, an early Middle English trea-

tise on the ascetical life: "The fiend beholds all this game: laughs till he bursts" (ed. M. Day, EETS.OS, 225 [1952]), 93–95.

6. Russell Fraser, *The War against Poetry* (Princeton, N.J.: Princeton University Press, 1970), 93–95; Jonas Barish, *The Antitheatrical Prejudice* (Berkeley, Los Angeles, and London: University of California Press, 1981), 91–92.

7. David Ormerod and Christopher Wortham, eds., *Dr. Faustus: The A-Text* (Nedlands, W. Aust.: Western Australia University Press, 1985), 52, trace "*Homo fuge*" to 1 Timothy 6.11–12 ("But thou, o man of God, flee from these things, and follow after righteousness, godlines, faith, love, pacience, & meeknes. Fight the good fight of faith: laye hold of eternal life." They suggest that "Whither should I fly?" is an echo of Psalm 139.7–8.

8. *Marlowe's "Doctor Faustus" 1604–1616*, ed. W. W. Greg (Oxford: Clarendon Press, 1950), B text, line 553; hereafter cited as "Greg."

Chapter 8

1. Michael Mangan, *Marlowe: "Doctor Faustus"* (London: Penguin Books, 1987), 61–73.

2. *English Moral Interludes*, ed. Glynne Wickham (London: Dent, 1976), 7–11.

3. Richard Levin, *The Multiple Plot in English Renaissance Drama* (Chicago and London: Chicago University Press, 1971), ch. 4.

4. See my "Comedy and Terror in Middle-English Literature: The Diabolical Game," *Modern Language Review* 60 (1965): 323–32.

5. At this point, one is tempted to reconsider the theory that B is not an amplification of A, but rather that A is a shortened version of B made for a touring company without the resources for spectacle available in the London theater. However, I have said I would sidestep that dispute.

Chapter 9

1. *"Everyman" and Medieval Miracle Plays*, ed. A. C. Cawley (New York: Dutton; London: Dent, 1977).

2. See my article, "Magic, Fate, and Providence in Medieval Narrative and Sir Gawain and the Green Knight," *Review of English Studies* 16 (1965): 121–24.

3. Robert Potter, *The English Morality Play* (London and Boston: Routledge, 1973), 126.

4. See *The Book of Sundials*, ed. H. K. F. Eden and Eleanor Lloyd, 3d ed. (London: Bell, 1890); cited in *"Dr. Faustus": The A-Text*, 158.

5. Everyman ed., 3.404 (pt. 3, sec. 4, mem. 2, subs. 4).

6. From a list of titles given in Wilbur Sanders, *The Dramatist and the Received Idea* (Cambridge: Cambridge University Press, 1968), 246–47.

7. *The Two Books of Homilies Appointed to be Read in Churches*, ed. J. Griffiths (Oxford: Oxford University Press, 1859), 78–79.

8. Martin Del Rio, *Les Controverses et recherches magiques*, vol. 2 (Paris, 1611), 4; cited in M. Garçon and J. Vinchon, *The Devil: An Historical Critical, and Medical Study*, trans. S. H. Guest, 6th ed. (London: Gollancz, 1929), 74.

9. *The Persecutory Imagination: English Puritanism and the Literature of Religious Despair* (Oxford: Clarendon Press, 1991), 293.

10. On the play as subversively predestinarian, see Michael Keefer, ed., *Christopher Marlowe's "Doctor Faustus": A 1604-Version Edition* (Peterborough, Ontario: Broadview Press, 1991), xiii–xxii, xlvii–xlviii. Keefer acknowledges a debt to Jonathan Dollimore's *Radical Tragedy*.

11. Edgar C. S. Gibson, *The Thirty-nine Articles of the Church of England, Explained with an Introduction* (London: Methuen, 1910), 459–60.

12. See Charles Hardwick, *A History of the Articles of Religion* (Cambridge: Deighton; London: Rivington, 1851), 155–73; V. J. K. Brook, *Whitgift and the English Church* (London: English Universities Press, 1959), 158–65; P. J. Lake, "Calvinism and the English Church," *Past and Present* 114 (1987): 46–49.

13. See, for example, H. D. F. Kitto, *Greek Tragedy* (London: Methuen, 1939), 139: "Oedipus is not being given his deserts by an offended heaven. What happens is the natural result of the weaknesses and virtues of his character, in combination with other peoples'. . . . Sophocles is not trying to make us feel that an inexorable destiny or a malignant god is guiding events." Cf. C. M. Bowra, *Sophoclean Tragedy* (Oxford: Clarendon Press, 1944): "His doom is fixed [by the gods] before his birth" (167). "His fate is not deserved; it is not . . . due to any fault of judgement or character" (175).

Bibliography

Primary Works

"*Everyman*" *and Medieval Miracle Plays*. Edited by A. C. Cawley. New York: Dutton; London: Dent, 1977.

The History of the Damnable Life and Deserved Death of Doctor John Faustus, Modernized and edited by William Rose. London: Routledge; New York: Dutton, n.d. [1925].

Kramer, Heinrich, and James Sprenger. *The Malleus Maleficarum*. Translated by Montague Summers. London: Rodtker, 1928.

Materials toward a History of Witchcraft. 3 vols. Edited by Henry Charles Lea. New York and London: Yoseloff, 1957. European witchcraft from early Christian times until the nineteenth century. Selections from original writings, with editorial commentary.

Mankind, in *English Moral Interludes*. Edited by Glynne Wickham. Totowa, N.J.: Rowman and Littlefield; London: Dent, 1976.

Marlowe, Christopher. *Doctor Faustus: A and B Text*. Edited by David Bevington and Eric Rasmussen. New Revels Series. Manchester: Manchester University Press, 1993. Gives both the A and the B texts in their entirety. Promises to become the most authoritative modern edition of *Faustus*.

——. *Doctor Faustus*. Edited by Roma Gill. New Mermaid Series. 2d edition. London: Black; New York: Norton, 1989. Compact edition based on the A text. Good notes.

——. *Doctor Faustus*. Edited by Roma Gill. Volume 2 of *Marlowe's Complete Works* (in progress). Oxford: Clarendon Press, 1990. The A text, with appendices containing substantial excerpts from *The Damnable Life* and the B text "additions."

———. *Doctor Faustus 1604–1616: Parallel Texts.* Edited by W. W. Greg. Oxford: Clarendon Press, 1959. Old-spelling edition of both A and B on facing pages.

———. *Doctor Faustus: A 1604-Version Edition.* Edited by Michael Keefer. Peterborough, Ontario: Broadview Press, 1991. Has useful appendices containing material from Calvin and *The Damnable Life.*

———. *"Dr Faustus": The A-Text.* Edited by David Ormerod and Christopher Wortham. Nedlands, W. Aust.: University of Western Australia Press, 1985. Excellent line-by-line annotation of the text. No scene or act divisions.

Palmer, Philip Mason, and Robert Pattison More. *The Sources of the Faust Tradition.* New York: Oxford University Press, 1936. Invaluable. Includes all of *The Damnable Life.*

Scot, Reginald. *The Discoverie of Witchcraft* (1587). Edited by Montague Summers. London: Rodker, 1930.

Woodes, Nathaniel. *The Conflict of Conscience* (1581). Oxford: Malone Society, 1952. Facsimile reprint.

Secondary Works

Bibliographies

Chan, Lois Mai, assisted by S. A. Pedersen. *Marlowe Criticism: A Bibliography.* Boston: G. K. Hall, 1978.

Friedenreich, Kenneth. *Christopher Marlowe: An Annotated Bibliography of Criticism since 1950.* Metuchen, N.J.: Scarecrow Press, 1979.

Kimbrough, Robert. "Christopher Marlowe." In Terence P. Logan and Denzell S. Smith, eds., *The Predecessors of Shakespeare: A Survey and Bibliography of Recent Studies in English Renaissance Drama.* Lincoln: University of Nebraska Press, 1973, 3–55.

Post, Jonathan F. S. "Recent Studies of Marlowe (1968–76)." *English Literary Renaissance* 7 (1977): 382–99.

Books

Bevington, David. *From "Mankind" to Marlowe: Growth and Structure in the Popular Drama of Tudor England.* Cambridge, Mass.: Harvard

Bibliography

University Press, 1962. Excellent chapter on *Faustus, The Conflict of Conscience*, and the morality tradition.

Bloom, Harold, ed. *Christopher Marlowe's "Doctor Faustus."* New York: Chelsea House, 1988. Good selection of recent essay-length studies. Complements the Farnham and Jump collections.

Boerner, Peter, and Sidney Johnson, eds. *Faust through Four Centuries.* Tubingen: Max Niemeyer Verlag, 1989. A symposium of lectures on varied aspects of the Faust legend.

Brockbank, Philip. *Marlowe: "Doctor Faustus."* London: Arnold, 1962. A learned and critically acute short study.

Butler, E. M. *The Fortunes of Faust.* Cambridge: Cambridge University Press, 1952. The origins and mutations of the Faust legend.

Cole, Douglas. *Suffering and Evil in the Plays of Christopher Marlowe.* Princeton, N.J.: Princeton University Press, 1962. Stresses Marlowe's theological education, his exploitation of human suffering, and his fascination with evil.

Dollimore, Jonathan. *Radical Tragedy: Religion, Ideology and Power in the Drama of Shakespeare and His Contemporaries.* Brighton: Harvester Press, 1984. A vigorously argued Marxist study that stresses the politically subversive and historically specific aspects of Renaissance tragedy.

Farnham, Willard, ed. *Twentieth-Century Interpretations of "Doctor Faustus."* Englewood Cliffs, N.J.: Prentice-Hall, 1969. Essays and excerpts including Santayana, Bradbrook, James Smith, Helen Gardner, Levi, Cole, Kirschbaum, Steane, and L. C. Knights.

Greenblatt, Stephen. *Renaissance Self-Fashioning: From More to Shakespeare.* Chicago and London: Chicago University Press, 1980. An influential study of Renaissance literature as reflecting a conflict in the shaping of personal identity between individual autonomy and cultural determination.

Heninger, S. K., Jr. *The Cosmographical Glass: Renaissance Diagrams of the Universe.* San Marino, Calif.: Huntington Library, 1977.

Hunter, Robert G. *Shakespeare and the Mystery of God's Judgements.* Athens: University of Georgia Press, 1976. Chapters on *The Conflict of Conscience* and *Faustus.* Argues that Calvinists, moderate Anglicans, and Catholics could all have seen in *Faustus* a confirmation of their respective views on sin and damnation.

Jump, John D., ed. *Marlowe, "Doctor Faustus": A Casebook.* London: Macmillan, 1969. Selected criticism: short extracts, 1817–1946; essay-length extracts, 1939–66. Very useful.

Kernan, Alvin, ed. *Two Renaissance Mythmakers: Christopher Marlowe and Ben Jonson.* Baltimore: Johns Hopkins University Press, 1971.

Levin, Harry. *The Overreacher: A Study of Christopher Marlowe.* Cambridge, Mass.: Harvard University Press, 1952. Marlowe's plays all dramatize an Icarian conflict between ideals and reality. Still perhaps the best book on Marlowe.

Mangan, Michael. *Marlowe: "Doctor Faustus."* London: Penguin Books, 1987. Valuable scene-by-scene analysis of the play, with introductory chapter on Marlowe's theater.

Mebane, John S. *Renaissance Magic and the Return of the Golden Age.* Lincoln: University of Nebraska Press, 1989. Compares the treatment of magic in Marlowe's *Faustus*, Jonson's *The Alchemist*, and Shakespeare's *The Tempest.*

Rozett, Martha Tuck. *The Doctrine of Election and the Emergence of Elizabethan Tragedy.* Princeton, N.J.: Princeton University Press, 1984. Chapter on *Faustus* stresses the play's theological ambiguities.

Sanders, Wilbur. *The Dramatist and the Received Idea: Studies in the Plays of Marlowe and Shakespeare.* Cambridge: Cambridge University Press, 1968. Offers a forcefully argued predestinarian interpretation of *Faustus.*

Smeed, J.W. *Faust in Literature.* London: Oxford University Press, 1975. Deals with various aspects of the Faust legend not treated in detail before.

Steane, J. B. *Marlowe: A Critical Study.* Cambridge: Cambridge University Press, 1964. Lively, detailed, New Critical analyses of the plays. Anticipates the current preference for the A text.

Tydeman, William. *"Doctor Faustus": Text and Performance.* London: Macmillan, 1984. Part 1 provides a critical introduction to the play; Part 2 considers some recent productions. A nicely balanced short study.

Tydeman, William, and Vivien Thomas. *Christopher Marlowe: A Guide through the Critical Maze.* Bristol: Bristol University Press, 1989. Summary and analysis of the criticism of each play. Extremely useful.

Articles and Chapters in Books (excluding those mentioned in footnotes)

Bluestone, Max. *"Libido Speculandi*: Doctrine and Dramaturgy in Contemporary Interpretations of *Doctor Faustus."* In Norman Rabkin, ed., *Reinterpretations of Elizabethan Drama: Selected Papers of the English Institute, 1968.* New York: Columbia University Press, 1969. Takes the concept of ambivalence as far as it will go in order to negotiate between interpretations of the play as orthodox or heterodox.

Cole, Douglas. "The Impact of Goethe's *Faust* on Nineteenth- and Twentieth-Century Criticism of Marlowe's *Doctor Faustus."* In Boerner and Johnson, *Faust through Four Centuries,* 185–96.

Bibliography

Deats, Sarah. "*Doctor Faustus*: From Chapbook to Tragedy." *Essays in Literature* 3 (1) (1976): 3–16. Examines the relationship between the play and its source, focusing on significant alterations.

Fisch, Harold. "The Pact with the Devil." *Yale Review* 69 (1980): 520–32. A wide-ranging survey of the myth which sees it as essentially Christian.

Jensen, Enjer J. "Heroic Convention and *Doctor Faustus*." *Essays in Criticism* (1971): 21, 101–6. Attempts to explain in what sense Faustus can be deemed heroic.

Kiessling, Nicholas. "*Doctor Faustus* and the Sin of Demoniality." *Studies in English Literature* 15 (1975): 205–11. Argues against W. W. Greg's view that Faustus is damned because of his sexual intercourse with "Helen."

Levin, Harry. "A Faustian Typology." In Boerner and Johnson, *Faust through Four Centuries*, 1–12. Examines the protean shapes of the myth.

Sachs, Arieh. "The Religious Despair of Doctor Faustus." *Journal of English and Germanic Philology* 63 (1964): 625–47. Faustus, probably a reprobate, is damned because of the sin of despair.

Sieferth, Howard. "The Concept of the Devil and the Myth of the Pact in Literature Prior to Goethe." *Monatschafte* 44 (1952): 271–89.

Watt, Ian. "Faust as a Myth of Modern Individualism: Three of Marlowe's Contributions." In Boerner and Johnson, *Faust through Four Centuries*, 41–52.

West, Robert H. "The Impatient Magic of Dr. Faustus." *English Literary Renaissance* 4 (1974): 218–40. A knowledge of Elizabethan magic, argues West, suggests that although the play has a heroic dimension, it is primarily moral.

Index

Index

Lucifer, 9, 24, 28, 117n6
Lust: and witchcraft, 39–43,

Magic: black and white, 33–5
Malleus Maleficarum (Sprenger and Kramer), 40, 45
Mangan, 86, 120n1
Mankind, 87–8
Mann, Thomas: *Doctor Faustus*, 11
Marxism, 18, 19, 63, 65
Middleton, Thomas, and William Rowley, *The Changeling*, 9, 10
Milton, John: *Samson Agonistes*, 85
Morality drama, 16, 30, 87, 97
Mythology, classical, 41, 54

Necromancy/negromancy, spelling of, 117n8
New Criticism, 16–18, 39
New historicism, 18–19, 63–4,
Nietzsche, 11, 64, 66

Oedipus, 112, 121n13
Ormerod, David, 116n4, 120n7
Ornstein, Robert, 16

Pact, demonic, 9, 23, 51, 97–8. *See also* Deed
Paganism. *See* Idolatry
Paul: Epistle to the Romans, 27, 50–1, 54
Plato: *Timaeus*, 56, 102
Popular tradition: in the *Damnable Life*, 29, 117
Predestination, 5–6, 17, 18, 106–112
Prometheus, 49–60
Puns, 48, 53, 54, 59, 72, 78–9, 83, 98. *See also* Deed
Puritans, 6–7, 69

Reformation, 4–6
Renaissance, 4–5, 7

Reprobation, 6. *See also* Predestination
Resolution: the heroic quality in Marlowe's plays, 13, 81–3
Rhetoric: and drama, 5
Role theory, 63, 65, 66

Sales, Roger, 65, 67, 119n3
Sanders, Wilbur, 17, 121
Santayana, George, 13
Scot, Reginald: *The Discoverie of Witchcraft*, 32
Sedgwick, G. C., 31
Sewall, R. B., 117n9
Shakespeare, 9, 10, 13, 52; *Macbeth*, 44; *Julius Caesar*, 44
Shepherd, Simon, 64–5, 84, 119n2
Smith, James, 15
Spengler, Oswald: *Decline of the West*, 11
Spies, Johann: *Historia von D. Johann Fausten*, 23
Spira, Francis, 15, 16, 17
Stachniewski, John, 108
States, Bert O., 117n8
Steane, J. B., 17
Swinburne, A. C., 12–13
Symonds, J. A., 13

Tamburlaine the Great (Christopher Marlowe), 13, 14, 36, 62, 66, 86
Theatricality, 5, 62–84. *See also* Drama
Three: the number of witchcraft, 51–2
Time, 87, 101, 102–105
Tragedy, 16, 27, 30–31, 42–3, 85 6, 96, 112–113, 118n12, 121
Tydeman, William, 116n16

Wagner, Wilhelm, 13
Wilson, F. P., 15, 16

131

The Author

Thomas McAlindon is professor of English at the University of Hull, England. His published research extends over a wide area, from Greek and medieval romance to the poetry of W. B. Yeats and the novels of Joseph Conrad, but his main interest is in Renaissance drama. Among his chief publications in this area are *Shakespeare and Decorum* (1973), *English Renaissance Tragedy* (1986), and *Shakespeare's Tragic Cosmos* (1991).

(continued from front flap)

Along the way, McAlindon blends new insights with contributions by major critics—from the Romantics to the postmoderns—to consider the play's most powerful questions: Why does Faustus choose necromancy over religion? Could he have been saved? Did Marlowe write his final punishment as a moral lesson or as a human tragedy? The answers, as McAlindon unveils them, enrich not only our appreciation of Marlowe's play but also our understanding of Reformation thought and its legacy over four centuries.

The Author

T. McAlindon is professor of English at the University of Hull, England. His published research extends over a wide area, from Greek and medieval romance to the poetry of Yeats and the novels of Conrad, but his main interest is in Renaissance drama. Among his chief publications in this area are *Shakespeare and Decorum* (1973), *English Renaissance Tragedy*, and *Shakespeare's Tragic Cosmos* (1991).